Hofmannsthal and Symbolism

American University Studies

Series III
Comparative Literature

Vol. 18

PETER LANG
New York · Berne · Frankfurt am Main

Thomas A. Kovach

Hofmannsthal and Symbolism

Art and Life in the Work of a Modern Poet

PETER LANG
New York · Berne · Frankfurt am Main

Library of Congress Cataloging in Publication Data

Kovach, Thomas A.
Hofmannsthal and Symbolism.

(American University Studies. Series III.
Comparative Literature; vol. 18)
Based on the author's thesis (Princeton University).
Bibliography: p.
Includes index.
1. Hofmannsthal, Hugo von, 1874–1929 – Criticism
and interpretation.   2. Symbolism (Literary movement)
3. Aestheticism (Literature)   4. French poetry –
19th century – History and criticism.   I. Title.
II. Series: (American University Studies.   Series III.
Comparative Literature; v. 18)
   PT2617.047Z73994   1986   831'.912   85-9947
   ISBN 0-8204-0240-0
   ISSN 0724-1445

CIP-Kurztitelaufnahme der Deutschen Bibliothek

Kovach Thomas A.:
Hofmannsthal and Symbolism: Art and Life in the
Work of a Modern Poet / Thomas A. Kovach. –
New York; Berne; Frankfurt am Main: Lang, 1985.
   (American University Studies: Ser. 3, Comparative
   Literature; Vol. 18)
   ISBN 0-8204-0240-0

NE: American University Studies / 03

© Peter Lang Publishing, Inc., New York 1985

All rights reserved.
Reprint or reproduction, even partially, in all forms such as
microfilm, xerography, microfiche, microcard, offset strictly prohibited.

Printed by Lang Druck, Inc., Liebefeld/Berne (Switzerland)

For
my parents

TABLE OF CONTENTS

PREFACE ix
INTRODUCTION 1
CHAPTER ONE: THE IMPACT OF SYMBOLISM ON THE WORK OF
HOFMANNSTHAL'S "LYRICAL DECADE" 25

   Section One: "La Vie Antérieure" and "Präexistenz" . . 25

   Section Two: "Sprachskepsis und Sprachmagie" 47

   Section Three: A New Kind of Poetry 55

      A. "Die festen romanischen Formen" 63

      B. Dramatic Lyric and Lyrical Drama 74

CHAPTER TWO: THE RECONCILIATION OF POETRY AND LIFE . . . 99

   Section One: Aesthetes and Artists in the
             Lyrical Dramas 106

   Section Two: Art, Life, and Language in the Essays . 116

      A. Essays of the "Lyrical Decade" 116

      B. Chandos and Beyond: Essays of
         the Later Years 141

CHAPTER THREE: THE AFFIRMATION OF LIFE 169

   Section One: "Si la beauté n'était la
   mort . . .": Mallarmé's "Hérodiade" 170

   Section Two: Hofmannsthal and the Thematics
             of Fertility 191

      A. Elektra 194

      B. Die Frau ohne Schatten 204

CONCLUSION 235
BIBLIOGRAPHY 245
INDEX 259

PREFACE

As this book sees the light of day, I would like to express my thanks to a number of individuals. First to Theodore Ziolkowski, now Dean of the Graduate School at Princeton University, who supervised the writing of the work in its original form as a dissertation; his example as critic, teacher, and human being has been an inspiration to me throughout my career. Then to Ralph Freedman, Professor of Comparative Literature at Princeton, for some valuable suggestions in the early stages of writing, for his encouragement upon its completion, and for his help in recent days. Then to Clarence Brown and Robert Fagles, also members of the Princeton Department of Comparative Literature, for their positive response to the work in its earliest form.

Of those who have been involved in the transformation of this work from dissertation to book, I should like to thank Dorrit Cohn of Harvard University and Christa Saas of the University of Toronto for their advice, help, and encouragement. Then I would like to say a special word of thanks to my friend and colleague Bob Helbling of the University of Utah, to whom I owe more than I can say.

Of those critics from whose work I have profited, I would like to single out the late Peter Szondi, whose book on turn-of-the-century lyric drama was the single most influential secondary work in the evolution of my ideas, and whose work as teacher and critic in general has been a continuing inspiration to me.

I would like to thank Evalyn Sandberg of the University of Utah Telecommunications Department for some valuable stylistic suggestions, and for her competence and thoroughness in preparing this manuscript.

On a personal level, I want to thank my wife Ada Mae for her love and support; without her I don't know how I would have survived these past few years. And finally, I want to thank my parents, to whom this book is dedicated, for their love and encouragement at all times.

* * *

Portions of this work have appeared previously, in somewhat altered form, in <u>Comparative Literature</u> and <u>The German Quarterly</u>; I am grateful to the editors of those journals for their permission to reprint this material.

* * *

I prefer to let the work speak for itself, but I should mention that any aberrant spellings in the German quotes, particularly from Bahr and Hofmannsthal in the 1890s, may be assumed to reflect the idiosyncrasies of the original writers.

Salt Lake City, Utah
February 1985

INTRODUCTION

In an 1892 essay, the eighteen-year-old Hugo von Hofmannsthal wrote:

> Denn dazu, glaube ich, sind Künstler: daß alle Dinge, die durch ihre Seele hindurchgehen, einen Sinn und eine Seele empfangen. . . . Und manche Wolken, schwere goldengeballte, haben ihre Seele von Poussin, und manche, rosigrunde, von Rubens, und andere, prometheische, blauschwarze, düstere, von Böcklin.[1]

One could almost guess in what decade these lines were written; the assertion of art's superiority to nature, the refusal to view nature except through an artist's eyes, are the standard fare of the Aestheticism of the 1890s. Hofmannsthal's statement here is strikingly similar to the views of Oscar Wilde, as expressed in his dialogue "On the Decay of Lying." And yet, in the very same year Hofmannsthal opened his essay "Südfranzösische Eindrücke" by speaking approvingly of

> . . . der unabsichtlichen Anmut, die das Leben hat. Denn die Bilder des Lebens folgen ohne inneren Zusammenhang aufeinander und ermängeln gänzlich der effektvollen Komposition.[2]

Though the second sentence could have been spoken by Wilde, the first makes it clear that what was chaotic and distasteful to Wilde was graceful and pleasing to Hofmannsthal.

The attempt to understand the ambivalence displayed by the young poet in these two passages leads one into some of the central problems posed by Hofmannsthal's work, problems which his critics, for the most part, have failed to deal with satisfactorily. Most of Hofmannsthal's contemporaries viewed him as the "aesthetic" poet par excellence, and they had no comprehension or sympathy for his later attempts to break out of and destroy the Aestheticist shell which had enclosed him during his early years. In contrast, most recent critics have gone to the other extreme, dealing only with the poet's critique of Aestheticism and failing to account for the fact that most of his early literary and artistic influences came from people who could be included under the banner of Aestheticism, in particular the major poets of French Symbolism.

In the following pages I propose to examine Hofmannsthal's relationship to the Symbolist movement, an endeavor which will enable us to see how the poet resolved this ambivalence, in his work as poet and as critic, and which will also cast a new light on his work and on his place in literary history. To the extent that this relationship took the form of a positive influence, we will be concerned primarily with the poets Charles Baudelaire, Paul Verlaine, and Stéphane Mallarmé; in discussing the negative aspects of this relationship, the poet's critique of the Aestheticist Weltanschauung, we will broaden our scope to include writers who are neither French nor Symbolists, in any strict sense of the term.

Since the term "Symbolism" is one which is used in many divergent senses, I should like to specify here that I use the term essentially to refer to the major poets listed above, rather than to the younger generation of poets in the 1880s and 1890s who first used the term "Symbolisme" and who took these three predecessors as their literary mentors -- Jean Moréas, author of the Symbolist Manifesto of 1886, René Ghil, Gustave Kahn, Jules Laforgue, and many others. Even so, the inclusion of Baudelaire in a discussion of Symbolism perhaps requires some justification; after all, he was one generation removed from the Symbolist masters Mallarmé and Verlaine, and two generations from the poets of the 1880s and 1890s. And yet there is hardly any tendency of Symbolism which does not find its source in the work of Baudelaire, most notably the doctrine of "correspondances" from Baudelaire's sonnet of the same name, which formed one of the mainstays of Symbolist aesthetics. Thus it is not surprising that he is included in most discussions of Symbolism as a major European literary movement, as opposed to a short-lived phase in the history of French poetry.[3]

To the extent that the Symbolist influence on Hofmannsthal's work has been acknowledged, however reluctantly, by critics, it has often been asserted that this influence was decisive during his "lyrical decade" of the 1890s, but that it was abandoned after the "Chandoskrise" of 1902 as the poet turned away from lyric poetry to the more public forms of his later years.[4] And yet this schema is false on two counts. First of all, the second passage quoted above shows the poet as early as 1892 praising the haphazardness of natural images as opposed to the artificial "composition" favored by the writers of Symbolism and Aestheticism. Indeed, a study of the poetry, lyric dramas, and essays of this early period reveals a deep and nearly constant preoccupation with the dilemma of a detached and noncommittal "aesthetic" existence, which is always viewed negatively. At the same time, there can be no question of Hofmannsthal's ever renouncing completely these early influences; in his "Gespräch über Gedichte," written <u>after</u> the Chandos letter, he makes his most explicit statement of Symbolist aesthetics. Indeed, probably the most valuable accomplishment of recent Hofmannsthal criticism has been to show the essential continuity that exists in the poet's work as a whole; the forms may change, but the essential concerns remain the same from the beginning to the end of his career.

* * *

It may be useful at this point to survey what we know about Hofmannsthal's acquaintance with the work of the French Symbolists in his early years. It is probably safe to assume that Hofmannsthal's intensive study of the Symbolists began only after his meeting with Stefan George in December of 1891, but there are several factors which make it likely that the young poet had had at least some exposure to Symbolist writings prior to this meeting, and even prior to his meeting with Hermann Bahr in April of the same year. First of all, the poet demonstrated even in his very first essays a thorough knowledge of contemporary European literature which was astonishing in someone his age; his letters of this period also testify to the breadth and diversity of his reading. Secondly, he was universally acknowledged to be a superior student of languages, and in particular he was a prize pupil of Gabriel Dubray, a noted French teacher and author of several books on the French language, in whose company Hofmannsthal made his trip to Southern France in the summer of 1892.[5] Furthermore, Hermann Bahr had made reference to Baudelaire, Verlaine, and Mallarmé in an essay on the Parnassiens in the first series of essays entitled Zur Kritik der Moderne,[6] to which Hofmannsthal refers familiarly in his 1891 essay on Bahr's novel Die Mutter, the essay which caused Bahr to seek out the young man's acquaintance. Finally, at least three critics[7] have heard echoes of Baudelaire in certain passages of his first lyrical drama Gestern (1891), most notably Andrea's speech praising mendacity and sin.[8] This last point is interesting, for it suggests that Hofmannsthal at this time saw Baudelaire mainly in his aspect as Satanist, decadent, dandy, and épateur of the bourgeois, not yet recognizing in him the serious and supremely great artist. In the essay on Bahr's novel Die Mutter Hofmannsthal speaks of "Baudelairismus" as a kind of dilettantism which seeks the "Darstellung des Angelebten"[9] -- angelebt is a rather uncommon word, but it seems to be used here in the sense of a life which is lived vicariously, and thus Baudelaire is seen as exemplifying the form of decadence characterized by detachment and alienation from life.

In early 1891, Hermann Bahr returned to Vienna, and there he sought to learn more about the mysterious "Loris" whose review of Bahr's own novel had revealed such literary sophistication. One can imagine his astonishment at learning that "Loris" was no middle-aged, widely-travelled Frenchman, as Bahr suspected, but rather a seventeen-year-old student at the Akademisches Gymnasium who had adopted the pseudonym largely because the rules of his school forbade its students to publish. Hofmannsthal had been introduced into the literary circle at the Cafe Griensteidl the previous year by Gustav Schwarzkopf, and it was there that Bahr met Hofmannsthal.

Bahr, who during the course of his career was the apostle of a long series of "isms," was at the time an undiscriminating admirer of all things French. About half of the essays in the above-mentioned first series of Zur Kritik der Moderne, though addressed to a German-speaking public, concern the contemporary scene in Paris. Thus Bahr can be assumed to have been thoroughly conversant in the names of French artists, movements, slogans, and journals, and it is certainly possible that he gave Hofmannsthal the incitement to read further in the French literature of the day and of the recent past, thus possibly including the works of the Symbolist masters Baudelaire, Verlaine, and Mallarmé. But is it likely that Bahr was able to give Hofmannsthal any new insight into this literature? To answer this question we must turn to Bahr's own writings, specifically his essays on "Die Décadence" and "Symbolisten" in the new series of Studien zur Kritik der Moderne[10] published in 1894 (though some were written earlier), as well as the essay on "Les Parnassiens" in the 1890 series. Without going beyond the titles, we can see that Bahr tended to latch on to every new school, every new slogan that was in the air; even when (as is rare) he deals with a particular author, he will try to "define" him in these terms, as when he calls Villiers de l'Isle-Adam "der letzte Romantiker und der erste Décadent"[11] or refers to Huysmans' "idealistischer Naturalismus."[12] In contrast, Bahr himself hailed Hofmannsthal as a critic for his indifference to such terms:

> Da war endlich einmal einer, der nicht nach abgegrasten Phrasen, nicht nach den Schlagworten der Schulen . . . sprach, sondern in den Künstler ging, auf seine wirren Dränge horchte und an ihrem Maasse seine Kunst entschied.[13]

Thus it is unlikely that Bahr won Hofmannsthal over to his enthusiasm for all the latest schools and slogans.

Let us turn now to the content of these essays. In "Les Parnassiens" Bahr gives a reasonably accurate assessment of these poets, emphasizing their devotion to the perfection of artistic form, which was derived in turn from the doctrine of l'art pour l'art in Gautier and Baudelaire, and he points out the indebtedness of nearly all the more recent French poets to

their efforts. It is here that he makes reference to "Paul
Verlaine, der nur im Schaurigen heiter ward" and "Stephane
Malarmé [sic] mit der priesterlichen Geberde und der dunklen
Rede, der immer rätseliger und mystischer wurde, der Vater der
Décadents."[14] Though the essay bears witness to Bahr's
talent for presenting sympathetically the personalities and
aspirations of artists, it gives no sign of any deeper insight
into their works; the descriptions of Verlaine and Mallarmé
are of the sort that could be found in numerous Parisian
journals of the day. Thus all that Hofmannsthal could have
learned from this are the names and descriptions of the poets
discussed; but since Hofmannsthal himself had in 1891 printed
a eulogy to Théodore de Banville, who is considered a primary
influence on at least one strain of Parnassianism,[15] Hofmannsthal most likely already knew of these poets.

If we consider the essays on "Die Décadence" and "Symbolisten" brought together in the 1894 Studien zur Kritik der
Moderne (at least one had appeared elsewhere as early as
1892),[16] the results are no more enlightening. One looks in
vain for any clear distinction between the terms; Bahr himself
seems to imply that they are merely two names for the same
artists, the same tendency, leaving open the question as to
why he treats them separately. Few names are mentioned; he
cites Maupassant's Roger de Salin and Huysmans' Des Esseintes
as fictional characters who illustrate the decadent preference
for the artificial, and the major French Symbolists are men-

tioned only in a list of Des Esseintes' favorite authors. The "Symbolisten" essay mentions no names of contemporary writers, but at the end presents two poems as "handliche Schulbeispiele" of Symbolism -- not French poems, but instead two minor compositions by Hofmannsthal!

In spite of this lack of specific reference, there is little doubt that the writers Bahr had in mind were not the major figures a modern reader thinks of when the term Symbolism is mentioned -- Baudelaire, Verlaine, Mallarmé -- but rather the group of lesser poets who took these men as their models, and who claimed for themselves the titles of Symbolists, Decadents, and numerous other appellations during the course of the 1880s and 1890s. In the essay on "Die Décadence" Bahr does mention a number of the traits which characterize these authors as well as their greater predecessors: the depiction of the inner life, the inclination toward all things artificial, the passion for mysticism. Symbolism he describes as a technique:

> [Der neue Symbolismus] will auch ins Unsinnliche, aber er will es durch ein anderes Mittel . . . er will die Nerven in jene Stimmungen zwingen, wo sie von selber nach dem Unsinnlichen greifen, und will das durch sinnliche Mittel. Und er verwendet die Symbole als Stellvertreter und Zeichen nicht des Unsinnlichen, sondern von anderen ebenso sinnlichen Dingen.
> Die Absicht aller Lyrik ist immer die gleiche: ein Gefühl, eine Stimmung, ein Zustand des Gemüthes soll ausgedrückt und mitgetheilt, soll suggerirt werden. Was kann der Künstler thun? . . . [er] kann eine ganz andere

> Ursache, ein ganz anderes äusseres Ereignis finden, welche seinem Zustande ganz fremd sind, aber welche das nämliche Gefühl, die nämliche Stimmung erwecken und den nämlichen Erfolg im Gemüthe bewirken würden.[17]

This description may be applicable to some of the poetry written around this time, perhaps even to some of Verlaine's poetry. But to suggest that Mallarmé "uses" symbols to represent other sensuous objects is hardly an adequate description of his poetic technique. Bahr's conception of this art is entirely subjective and psychological; for him it is an art of the nerves, those of the poet and those of the reader. The transcendental, metaphysical element which is such an integral part of Mallarmé's work and that of other Symbolists is psychologized into "eine fieberische Sucht nach dem Mystischen." And the tendency towards objectification, towards the disappearance of the poetic subject, goes entirely unnoticed by Bahr.

The terms in which Bahr discusses writers in these and other essays reveal the extent to which he was attuned to the intellectual climate of Vienna around the turn of the century, the city of Freud and Schnitzler. Hofmannsthal himself, writing during this time, displays some of the same concerns, particularly in his essays on works by the contemporary French writers Paul Bourget, Henri-Frédéric Amiel, and Maurice Barrès. These works interest him precisely in their psychological preoccupation, in their analysis of the modern sensibility; and he speaks of them in terms which are often strikingly reminiscent of Bahr's essay; Barrès' work he calls "die Ethik der modernen Nerven."[18] But Hofmannsthal makes it clear that the work of these men cannot really be taken as art; after listing all of Amiel's gifts as a writer, he concludes with devastating effect: "Amiel hat zum großen Künstler nur eines gefehlt...: Können."[19] The ability to transcend the self and its complexities in the creation of a work of art is exactly what Hofmannsthal felt these writers lacked, and despite his very sympathetic account of the interest these works hold for the modern reader, he does not hesitate to point this out. If the essays of Bahr and this contemporary French writing taught Hofmannsthal anything, it was only by negative example. In an 1891 letter to Bahr, Hofmannsthal writes:

> Was Ihrer Kritik Farbe und Duft gibt, befremdet mich dort, wo Barrès, Bourget und unsre andren Meister der "psychologischen monologia" mich gelehrt haben, mein Pathos zu verlernen und auf lyrisme zu verzichten.[20]

If one reads through the letters that Hofmannsthal wrote to Bahr, it becomes clear that Hofmannsthal regarded Bahr's attachment to the Paris literary scene with some amusement, and that whatever his personal fondness for the older man, it was he whose literary judgments may have influenced Bahr, rather than the other way around.

This examination of the possible role of Bahr in

introducing the literature of French Symbolism to Hofmannsthal has served two purposes. First, we have seen that it is highly unlikely that Bahr "initiated" Hofmannsthal in any significant sense into the writings of the major Symbolist poets. But in addition, it is important to note Bahr's view of these poets, since he is widely considered to have been <u>the</u> apostle of French Symbolism in Vienna, and his views can be assumed to be fairly representative of the attitude of Viennese literary circles in the 1890s to the French movement. The comment on "Baudelairismus" quoted earlier suggests that at this time Hofmannsthal too made no distinction between the major Symbolists and their numerous and factious followers.

And yet, later in his life, Hofmannsthal in his self-interpretation <u>Ad me ipsum</u> began a list headed "Zeitpunkt 1892. Frühe Einflüsse." with the names of Poe, Baudelaire, Verlaine, and Mallarmé.[21] Clearly some change took place around this time, and the source of this change is not hard to find. In December of 1891, Stefan George, who was travelling through Europe in search of kindred spirits, came to Vienna and sought out young "Loris," one of whose already-published essays had convinced him that its author was "unter den wenigen in Europa . . . (und hier in Österreich der einzige) mit denen er Verbindung zu suchen habe."[22] This meeting was to be fateful for both men. For George, the exaltation he felt at having found at last (as he thought) the soulmate who would understand and appreciate his work and would himself create new poetry to equal it, was soon followed by the pain and frustration of seeing his "Zwillingsbruder" reject his advances. For Hofmannsthal, Stefan George opened up a new world. Previously surrounded by the writers of "Jung-Wien" with whom Hofmannsthal enjoyed friendly relations but whom he recognized as his inferiors as writers, Hofmannsthal was introduced by George to the works of living and recently dead poets who shared many of his aspirations and his serious devotion to the art of poetry, foremost among them the French Symbolists.

Unlike Bahr, George knew whereof he spoke. Upon his arrival in Paris in March of 1889, George had made the acquaintance of the poet Albert Saint-Paul, who moved in Symbolist circles and was a regular visitor to the Tuesday evening gatherings at Mallarmé's apartment on the Rue de Rome. Saint-Paul was able to acquaint George with the most important Symbolist writings (including those of Baudelaire, whom George began to translate around this time), and to bring George himself into the circle of those who gathered to hear the Master's words every Tuesday. George made his presence felt to the point of attracting the kindly interest of Mallarmé. After George had failed to appear one Tuesday, Mallarmé wrote to him: "Aussi désolé, pour ma part, que vous voulez bien l'être, mon cher George: nous aurions causé et de vous et de tous."[23] George later paid tribute to the French poets who had given him a poetic ideal to follow when none seemed to exist in his homeland: "VERLAINE in fall und busse fromm und kindlich / und für sein denkbild blutend: MALLARME."[24]

There is abundant evidence to suggest that the French Symbolists and their works formed a large part of the conversations between George and Hofmannsthal in the month between their meeting in mid-December 1891 and George's departure from Vienna in mid-January 1892. Hofmannsthal's diary entry for December 21 (presumably the day of their first meeting) reads: "Stefan George. (Baudelaire, Verlaine, Mallarmé, Poe, Swinburne.) 'Unsere Klassiker waren nur Plastiker des Stils, noch nicht Maler und Musiker.'" An entry for Christmas evening speaks of a visit by George, and refers to "l'Ermitage," one of the current Symbolist journals, and mentions a "Symbolistenstreit," the precise reference of which is unknown. An entry for January 9 reveals that the conversation revolved around Mallarmé's "l'Après-midi d'un faune," a handwritten copy of which George had presented to Hofmannsthal (Mallarmé's works were not widely available at the time) as well as George's own _Pilgerfahrten_. In a letter written to his friend, the Germanist Walther Brecht, shortly before his death in 1929, Hofmannsthal wrote of those times:

> Wir kamen dann einige Male zusammen: die Namen Verlaine, Baudelaire, Swinburne, Rossetti, Shelley, wurden dabei in einer gewissen Weise genannt -- man fühlte sich als Verbundene; auch der Name D'Annunzio kam schon vor und natürlich Mallarmé.[25]

In examining Hofmannsthal's relationship with George, we are dealing with precisely the opposite problem from that which confronted us in the case of Bahr. It is clear from their correspondence that Hofmannsthal and Bahr had a warm personal rapport from the start; but it is equally clear that Hofmannsthal regarded Bahr's literary views with amused detachment and was interested in his novels as <u>Zeiterscheinungen</u> rather than as serious works of art. In George, on the other hand, Hofmannsthal encountered for the first time a poet of genius, and one who did in fact teach the young poet a great deal; but his relationship with George was painfully uncomfortable from the very beginning, and was broken off in 1906 after a series of hopeless misunderstandings. The difference in temperament between the two men has been discussed so often that we need not examine it in detail. But since George was the only major Symbolist poet with whom Hofmannsthal came into personal contact until his meetings with Maeterlinck and Valéry some years later, it is possible that his reaction to George's personality may have colored his attitude towards Symbolism as a literary school, though it is unlikely to have affected his judgment of individual writers.

Nevertheless, as a result of his conversations with George, Hofmannsthal had revised his opinion of the Paris literary scene to the point of writing George a year later: "Ich bin Ihnen aufrichtig dankbar wenn Sie mir ein bischen [sic] Contact mit den Franzosen verschaffen, die unserer

Stimmung und Kunstweise nahverwandt sind."[26] It is clear from what follows that Hofmannsthal is referring here to the poets of his and George's own generation, not their older leaders. But a perusal of the Parisian journals in which these writers published their works caused Hofmannsthal to return to his original judgment:

> Die Bestrebungen der analogen französischen Hefte mit ihren Anlehnungen an die bildenden Künste, ihren gemachten Archaismen und Naivetäten waren mir immer recht sehr unerfreulich. Auch wird darin, soviel ich sehen kann, das inferiore vordringliche in gar keiner Zucht gehalten.[27]

Thus Hofmannsthal's new-found admiration for Baudelaire, Verlaine, and Mallarmé did not blind him to the fact that many of the same tendencies in the hands of lesser artists led to unfortunate results. This is a theme to which Hofmannsthal returns on several occasions. In some notes written on July 9, 1895, under the heading "Ästhetismus I," Hofmannsthal says:

> Große Anfänge, jetzige Depravation. -- Ein Kreislauf, sich wechselseitig steigernd, befruchtend-verderblich, zwischen England -- Belgien -- Frankreich. -- Künste neigen sich einander zu, entfernen sich vom Publikum, verderben schwächere Talente, welche die Emotion beim Genießen zum Nachproduzieren treibt.[28]

The "great beginnings" of Baudelaire, Verlaine, and Mallarmé are seen to have a destructive effect on lesser talents. In the same vein, Hofmannsthal in his essay on Francis Vielé-Griffin -- the only one of his essays specifically devoted to any of the French Symbolists -- speaks of the work of this American-born poet as being marred by its excessive reliance on Verlaine:

> Man muß sehr gut geboren sein, um die Existenz eines so komplexen und verführenden Künstlers, als Verlaine ist, zu ertragen, ohne von ihr unterworfen zu werden. . . . Ich sehe [Vielé-Griffins] Poesie beherrscht von dem undefinierbaren Rhythmus der Verlaineschen, von jenen süßen Verbindungen der Worte, von jenem unbegreiflichen Durcheinandergehen von Hingabe und Bemeisterung. Ich fühle den schwächlichen Versuch, jene unnachahmlichen Zeilen zu erreichen.[29]

Leopold Andrian, a close friend and fellow poet, reports that Verlaine was one of Hofmannsthal's favorite poets, and that he would jokingly say of him: "Dem mache ich so viel nach, wie ich kann."[30] Of course, this remark was not entirely in jest. Hofmannsthal knew that he was not one of the "schwächeren Talenten" and that his own poetic voice was strong enough to benefit from this influence without being undermined.

Several previously unpublished fragments from the Hofmannsthal papers in Houghton Library at Harvard University, made available in an article by Steven P. Sondrup, confirm the extent to which Hofmannsthal was immersed in the writings of the Symbolists, and even identified himself with the French movement.[31] Among these is a fragment from a longer letter to an unknown recipient, which is evidently a reply to a question as to the nature of Symbolism. This suggests that Hofmannsthal not only was regarded by his contemporaries, but also regarded himself during this period, as an authority on Symbolism. In this and in another fragment, Hofmannsthal lists several of his own works as examples of Symbolist poetry. Finally, he concludes the letter by referring to George, "der wirklich am meisten die Technik hat und auch persönlich die deutsche an die französische Bewegung bindet."[32]

Thus it is clear that whatever Hofmannsthal's knowledge of French Symbolist poetry may have been prior to meeting George in December 1891, it was only after and as a result of this meeting that Hofmannsthal began to study this writing in any depth. Indeed, in meeting George, he was presented with a unique opportunity to acquaint himself with these authors. George could give him a first-hand account of the aesthetics, devotion to art, and personal magnetism of Mallarmé; he could help the younger poet through some of the obscurities in the works of these poets, and could be for Hofmannsthal a living example of a German poet who followed the poetic ideals of the Symbolists.

* * *

This work will be divided into three major chapters. In the first, I will demonstrate the impact that Hofmannsthal's discovery of Symbolism exerted on the work of his "lyrical decade" from 1892 to 1900, including the lyrical dramas. Though it would be misleading to suggest that Hofmannsthal was ever totally uncritical in his attitude toward these writers (or any others, for that matter), it is in this period that their influence is the clearest. Though the critique of aestheticism which he was to carry on throughout his career was evident as early as the dramatic fragment Der Tod des Tizian of 1892, in these early years Hofmannsthal had not yet succeeded in reconciling his insight into the aesthetic and moral dangers of aestheticism with the fact that nearly all the living authors whom he most admired, notably the French Symbolists, were committed to the doctrine of l'art pour l'art in one form or another. The second chapter will be devoted to a study of Hofmannsthal's discursive attempts to resolve these problems posed by his Aestheticist-Symbolist heritage. The focus of attention here will be on Hofmannsthal's essays, though reference will be made to the lyrical dramas insofar as they raise some of the same problems. The third chapter will concentrate on Hofmannsthal's resolution of the problem in his art. Mallarmé's "Hérodiade," the greatest expression of the ideal of cold, sterile beauty so characteristic of the writers of Symbolism and Aestheticism, will be compared first with Hofmannsthal's Elektra, where this same sterile self-enclosure is revealed in its destructive and diseased aspects, and then with Die Frau ohne Schatten, where the values of commitment to the human community, self-denial, and fertility are held up as a counter-ideal to the tradition culminating in "Hérodiade." Finally, a concluding section will attempt to assess the poet

Hugo von Hofmannsthal and his work in its entirety, rejecting both the earlier view of him as an aesthete and the attempts of recent critics to portray him as a writer whose concerns are essentially social, in favor of a more balanced view of the poet as one who rejected aestheticism in its narrow, life-denying form but who revered the great masters of Symbolism and regarded the striving for artistic perfection as an ultimate value.

Notes

¹PI, pp. 75-76. All citations from Hofmannsthal's works are based on the Gesammelte Werke in Einzelausgaben, edited by Herbert Steiner and published from 1946 onward in Stockholm and Frankfurt by Fischer Verlag. Individual volumes will be abbreviated as follows:

E = Die Erzählungen (3rd edition)
GLD = Gedichte und lyrische Dramen (2nd edition)
PI = Prosa I
PII = Prosa II
PIV = Prosa IV
DII = Dramen II
DIII = Dramen III
A = Aufzeichnungen

²PI, p. 77

³See, for instance, René Wellek, "The Term and Concept of Symbolism in Literary History" in Discriminations (New Haven and London: Yale University Press, 1970), pp. 90-121.

⁴This is the tendency, for instance, of the most serious previous work devoted to the theme of Hofmannsthal and Symbolism, Steven P. Sondrup, Hofmannsthal and the French Symbolist Tradition (Bern: Herbert Lang, 1976).

⁵For more on Hofmannsthal's knowledge of French language and literature, consult Karl Foldenauer, "Hugo von

Hofmannsthal und die französische Literatur des 19. und 20. Jahrhunderts," Diss. Tübingen 1958.

[6]Hermann Bahr, Zur Kritik der Moderne: Erste Reihe (Zürich: Verlags-Magazin J. Schabelitz, 1890), p. 183.

[7]Ika Alida Thomèse, Romantik und Neuromantik mit besonderer Berücksichtigung Hugo von Hofmannsthals (The Hague: Martinus Nijhoff, 1923), p. 143; Enid Lowrie Duthie, L'influence du Symbolisme français dans le renouveau poétique de l'Allemagne (Paris: Honoré Champion, 1933), p. 424; Foldenauer, p. 106.

[8]GLD, p. 158.

[9]PI, p. 18.

[10]Hermann Bahr, Studien zur Kritik der Moderne (Frankfurt am Main: Rütten & Loening, 1894).

[11]Zur Kritik (1890), p. 195.

[12]Studien (1894), p. 98.

[13]Studien (1894), p. 123.

[14]Zur Kritik, p. 183.

[15]cf. Albert Thibaudet, French Literature from 1795 to Our Era, trans. Charles Lam Markmann (New York: Funk & Wagnalls, 1967), p. 295.

[16]"Symbolisten" published in Nation (Vienna: June 18, 1892).

[17]Studien, pp. 28-29.

[18]PI, p. 44.

[19]PI, pp. 29-30.

[20] Hugo von Hofmannsthal, <u>Briefe 1890-1901</u> (Berlin: Fischer Verlag, 1935), p. 29.

[21] <u>A</u>, p. 237.

[22] Quote taken from Hofmannsthal's letter to Walther Brecht, cited in Robert Boehringer, <u>Mein Bild von Stefan George</u>, 2nd ed. (Munich and Düsseldorf: Helmut Küpper, 1967), pp. 226-27.

[23] Boehringer, p. 31.

[24] Stefan George, <u>Gesamt-Ausgabe der Werke: Endgültige Fassung</u>, Vol. 6 (Berlin: Georg Bondi, 1931), p. 18

[25] Boehringer, p. 227.

[26] <u>Briefwechsel zwischen George und Hofmannsthal</u>, 2nd edition (Munich and Düsseldorf: Helmut Küpper, 1953), p. 50.

[27] <u>Briefwechsel</u>, p. 82.

[28] <u>A</u>, p. 123.

[29] <u>PI</u>, p. 221.

[30] Quoted in <u>Hugo von Hofmannsthal: Die Gestalt des Dichters im Spiegel seiner Freunde</u>, ed. Helmut Fiechtner (Vienna: Humboldt Verlag, 1953), p. 58.

[31] Steven P. Sondrup, "Three Notes on Symbolism by Hugo von Hofmannsthal," <u>Modern Austrian Literature</u>, 9, No. 2 (1976), 1-9.

[32] Sondrup, pp. 4-5.

CHAPTER ONE

THE IMPACT OF SYMBOLISM ON THE WORK
OF HOFMANNSTHAL'S "LYRIC DECADE"

Section One: "La Vie Antérieure" and "Praeexistenz"

Ever since 1930, when Walther Brecht published Ad me ipsum,[1] those notes which Hofmannsthal began in 1916 and completed in the early 1920s, and in which he attempted an interpretation of his own work up to that time, Hofmannsthal criticism has been dominated, often to an oppressive degree, by the attempt to fit all of the poet's writings into the schema and the terminology of this self-interpretation. In particular, countless words have been devoted to Hofmannsthal's use of the term Praeexistenz to designate the starting point, the first stage in the poet's development.

Hofmannsthal's own description of the term is sketchy. He refers to it as a "glorreicher, aber gefährlicher Zustand,"[2] immediately revealing the ambivalence with which this stage of development is viewed. Someone in this state is seen (or rather sees himself -- one can read it either way) as an "Angehöriger einer höchsten Welt," and in this connection he speaks of "millenarische Anklänge," thus suggesting the fundamental separation of this condition from everyday human existence, with even the suggestion of a terrestrial paradise. In this state the self sees no distinction between itself and the world, no boundaries to the self: "Das Ich als Universum."[3]

And yet the negative aspects of this state are immediately clear as well. On the one hand he refers to a "Geistige Souveränität: sieht die Welt von oben," and on the other he immediately suggests the consequence of this: "Nachteil: sieht nur Totalitäten,"[4] the inability, to reverse the saying, to see the trees for the forest. Ultimately this state cannot last, and the problem dealt with in <u>Ad me ipsum</u>, thus the problem which Hofmannsthal retrospectively saw as central to his life work, is how one makes the difficult transition from pre-existence into existence, into an active engagement with a world which has previously been experienced only intuitively and by anticipation.

The specific source of the term "Praeexistenz" in Hofmannsthal's usage has been established by two recent critics.[5] In his work <u>Kokoro</u>, first published in 1896, the Orientalist Lafcadio Hearn included a chapter entitled "The Idea of Preexistence," which deals with the significance of the concept in Japanese Buddhist thought and popular tradition. Hofmannsthal wrote an introduction for the 1905 German translation of this work; he recommended it to several of his friends, and a heavily annotated copy was found in his library after his death, so there can be no question about his thorough familiarity with the work.

Clearly, certain aspects of Japanese thought struck a deeply responsive chord in Hofmannsthal. The idea that each individual inherits the memory of the experiences of his ancestors is reflected in such lines as "Ganz vergessener Völker Müdigkeiten / Kann ich nicht abtun von meinen Lidern" from "Manche freilich. . . ." Hearn's emphasis on the Oriental conception of the self as an aggregate of many elements, as opposed to the Western notion of the discrete individual soul, is reflected in several notes from Ad me ipsum, such as "Das Ich als Universum . . . Gabe sich zu vervielfältigen."[6] But whereas the Oriental conception takes for granted an essential unity between the self and the world, Hofmannsthal saw the danger of the individual's absorbing the outer world into himself in his imagination, a form of self-aggrandizement suggested by the phrase "Das Ich als Universum" and characteristic of the Romantic poets whom Hofmannsthal regarded with some suspicion, largely for this reason. Where the Oriental might see the transition from pre-existence to existence as a passage from a totally collective state to an at least partly individuated form, Hofmannsthal saw this process as one of escape from a state of total self-enclosure into a sense of community with and commitment to one's fellow creatures.

Thus, although there can be no doubt as to where Hofmannsthal found the term "pre-existence," this does not imply that his usage of it coincides exactly with Hearn's. This being the case, it seems justified to consider other sources which may have influenced or which show some affinity to Hofmannsthal's conception.

In this section it is my intention to compare the concept of "Praeexistenz," as described in Ad me ipsum and reflected in some of the poems and lyric dramas, with a strain in Baudelaire exemplified in the poem "La Vie Antérieure" and elsewhere, and finally with a similar element in Mallarmé's early verse. The purpose is not to show a direct influence, though in the case of Baudelaire this is likely to have been the case, but rather to suggest some of the affinity among these poets.

* * *

Amidst the bleak urban landscape of Les Fleurs du Mal, there are a number of poems which suggest or depict states of being which stand in radical opposition to the dirt and degradation of mid-nineteenth century Paris. Usually the alternative is conceived spatially, in terms of a voyage of escape, although the voyage often results in further disillusionment:

> Le monde, monotone et petit, aujourd'hui,
> Hier, demain, toujours, nous fait voir notre
>   image:
> Une oasis d'horreur dans un désert d'ennui!
>   ("Le Voyage")

At such times, it seems there is no escape from the "désert d'ennui," at least not in the present. Thus, the only possibility which remains is an "escape" in time, not to any future utopia, but rather to the memory of a blissful state in the past. This is the subject of "La Vie Antérieure," a sonnet which appears early in the "Spleen et Idéal" section which opens Les Fleurs du Mal.

> J'ai longtemps habité sous de vastes portiques
> Que les soleils marins teignaient de mille feux,
> Et que leurs grands piliers, droits et majes-
>   tueux,
> Rendaient pareils, le soir, aux grottes basal-
>   tiques.
>
> Les houles, en roulant les images des cieux,
> Mêlaient d'une façon solennelle et mystique
> Les tout-puissants accords de leur riche musique
> Au couleur du couchant reflété par mes yeux.
>
> C'est là que j'ai vécu dans les voluptés calmes,
> Au milieu de l'azur, des vagues, des splendeurs,
> Et des esclaves nus, tout imprégnés d'odeurs,
>
> Qui me rafraîchissaient le front avec des
>   palmes,
> Et dont l'unique soin était d'approfondir
> Le secret douloureux qui me faisait languir.

The setting, to be sure, suggests spatial distance: a tropical isle, bright sun and blue sky, palms, naked slaves. Yet not only the title but also the first line of the first quatrain and that of the first tercet ("J'ai longtemps habité. . . . C'est là que j'ai vécu . . .") insist on this scene as one remembered from the past, not a dream vision engendered by a bleak present.

The first quatrain sets the scene. The poet lives beneath vast porticos which by day are illumined in fiery colors by the tropical sun. In the evening, the columns supporting the porticos help suggest basalt caves. The adjectives suggest size and majesty: the porticos are "vastes," the columns "droits et majestueux." It is perhaps worth noting that the Parisian poet envisioned, in even a tropical scene, porticos and columns -- figures of highly "civilized" urban architecture -- thus quickly undermining any sense of a Rouseauvian natural state. It is these artificial creations which suggest natural forms (basalt caves), and not the other way around.

The second quatrain is an example of the synesthesia of which Baudelaire and the later Symbolists were so fond. There are several elements at work here which it is impossible to distinguish clearly. First, the reflection of the sky is carried on the rolling waves, which in turn mingle their roaring sounds, "les tout-puissants accords de leur riche musique," with the reflection of the setting sun, this reflection not in the water, but in the poet's eyes. Thus the poet himself is caught up in a unity of sights and sounds. Whereas in the first quatrain, ensconced beneath the porticos, he seemed to contemplate his natural surroundings as a detached observer, here he seems at one with it all. His eyes, on the one hand, are mirrors which catch the colors of the sun and reflect them back onto the sea. On the other, they are the receptive organs which allow the poet to absorb the whole scene into himself. The majesty of the architecture in the first quatrain is carried over and intensified in the "solennelle et mystique" qualities of the ocean billows in the sunset.

The first two quatrains, though framed by personal references at beginning and end ("J'ai longtemps habité . . . par mes yeux"), deal essentially with the setting, which the poet observes in the first quatrain and is caught up in at the end of the second. The tercets, taking up where the second quatrain left off, focus squarely on the poet. The solemnity and majesty of his surroundings, both natural and man-made, give way to the "voluptés calme" as the poet basks amid the splendors of sea and sky, attended by naked slaves, their bodies soaked in perfumes, who fan his brow with palms. And yet this nineteenth-century decadent vision of tropical bliss is disturbed in the last two lines of the poem, where it is said that the slaves' only concern was to deepen "le secret douloureux qui me faisait languir."

It would be difficult to equate this "secret douloureux" with any specific knowledge on the part of the poet. Still, one must account for the impact of this phrase on the poem as a whole, and determine to what extent it negates or at least modifies what has come before. To begin with, it should be noted that despite the "civilized" elements introduced in the architecture of the first quatrain and in the perfumed slaves of the tercets, the poem up to this point has evoked the image of a natural paradise where one could live in a state of pure bliss, untouched by original sin or painful memories of any kind. And yet, in the final line Baudelaire suggests there is a painful secret which not only predates this former existence but in some way has caused it. Thus the poet confirms that there is no escape from suffering in time or space; as in "Un Voyage à Cythère," we are confronted at the end of the escape attempt with an image of suffering.

Still, can one really say that this final line overturns all that has come before, that the scene evoked in the major part of the poem is done so only to be undermined at the end? I think not. Though the parallel with "Un Voyage à Cythère" does suggest itself, there is a world of difference in tone and emphasis between the "secret douloureux" of this poem and the discovery of the poet's own likeness hanging from a tree on the isle of Cytherea. The secret has led, after all, not to any physical or mental agonies, but rather to the pleasant languishing, even the "voluptés calmes" described in the poem. We can find justification elsewhere in Baudelaire for regarding the word "douloureux" in an almost favorable light. In "Bénédiction," the opening poem of <u>Les Fleurs du Mal</u>, the poet, who is cursed and mocked by both mother and wife, casts his eye heavenward and proclaims:

> -- "Soyez béni, mon Dieu, qui donnez la souffrance
> Comme un divin remède à nos impuretés
> Et comme la meilleure et la plus pure essence
> Qui prépare les forts aux saintes voluptés!

Though the "voluptés" referred to here are those of an afterlife rather than a "vie anteriéure," the idea of suffering preparing the soul for delights to come seems strikingly similar. Two stanzas later, the poet goes on to say: "Je sais que la douleur est la noblesse unique / Où ne mordront jamais la terre et les enfers. . . ." Thus the "douloureux" of the concluding line, rather than undercutting what has come before, might even be seen as extending the air of majesty and nobility suggested by the architecture in the first quatrain and by the waves in the second, thus balancing and lending some dignity to the passive decadence evoked by the picture of the poet being attended by perfumed slaves.

And so the poem ends on a somewhat ambiguous note. It is as if the poet, fondly recalling a happier previous existence, is forced reluctantly to conclude that even this existence was not free of the painful awareness that is part of the human condition as Baudelaire found it, whether it is known as original sin or called by any other name. But this realization does not cancel out the memory. The possibility still stands of a happier -- indeed a luxuriantly self-indulgent -- life where even painful memories are a subtle cause of enjoyment.

Though the poem "La Vie Antérieure" represents the most explicit and detailed development of the idea of a happier past existence, it is by no means the only expression of this idea in Les Fleurs du Mal. In the opening poem "Bénédiction," quoted earlier, the following lines refer to the poet:

>   L'Enfant déshérité s'enivre de soleil,
>   Et dans tout ce qu'il boit et dans tout ce qu'il
>   mange
>   Retrouve l'ambroisie et le nectar vermeil.

Here the contrast of the poet's miserable life in the present with the memory of a happier time is apparent, though here the emphasis is on the unhappy present, the happier past being suggested only by the verb "retrouve" and its implication that the poet once did enjoy the nectar and ambrosia which he now can only imagine as he consumes his daily fare.

The tropical setting first introduced in "La Vie Antérieure" reappears several times in <u>Les Fleurs du Mal</u> in such poems as "L'Invitation au Voyage" and "A une Dame Créole," though without any explicit connection to a past existence. Even so, it could be argued that this connection is established in "La Vie Antérieure" and remains by implication in the later poems in the volume. In one poem, "Moesta et Errabunda," this tropical paradise, distant in space, is opposed to the joys of childhood, removed in time:

> Comme vous êtes loin, paradis parfumé,
> Où sous un clair azur tout n'est qu'amour et
>   joie.
> Où tout ce que l'on aime est digne d'être aimé,
> Où dans la volupté pure le coeur se noie!
> Comme vous êtes loin, paradis parfumé!
>
> Mais le vert paradis des amours enfantines,
> Les courses, les chansons, les baisers, les
>   bouquets,
> Les violons vibrant derrière les collines
> Avec les brocs de vin, le soir, dans les
>   bosquets,
> - Mais le vert paradis des amours enfantines,
>
> L'innocent paradis, plein de plaisirs furtifs,
> Est-il déja plus loin que l'Inde et que la
>   Chine?
> Peut-on le rappeler avec des cris plaintifs,
> Et l'animer encore d'une voix argentine,
> L'innocent paradis plein de plaisirs furtifs?

The answer to this question is clearly "no"; the past cannot be brought back; it is irretrievably lost and therefore more "distant" than India or China.

The idea of past joys lost forever leads directly to another, that of Time as destroyer. In the poem "L'Ennemi" the poet laments: "O douleur! ô douleur! Le Temps mange la vie. . . ." The opening section of Les Fleurs du Mal, "Spleen et Idéal," closes with the poem "L'Horloge" which deals with this same theme:

> Horloge! dieu sinistre, effrayant, impassible,
> Dont le doigt nous menace et nous dit: "Souviens toi!" . . .
>
> Le Plaisir vapoureux fuira vers l'horizon
> Ainsi qu'une sylphide, au fond de la coulisse;
> Chaque instant te dévore un morceau du délice
> A chaque homme accordé pour toute sa saison.

No one familiar with Hofmannsthal's work will fail to be reminded of the persistent theme of Vergänglichkeit, particularly in the early works. One need only recall the "Terzinen: Über Vergänglichkeit," with their lament:

> Wie kann das sein, daß diese nahen Tage
> Fort sind, für immer fort, und ganz vergangen?
>
> Dies ist ein Ding, das keiner voll aussinnt,
> Und viel zu grauenvoll, als daß man klage:
> Daß alles gleitet und vorüberrinnt.

or the Marschallin's famous monologue at the end of Act One of Der Rosenkavalier. Though this particular theme is probably as old as Western literature, certainly as old as Villon, its similar expression in the works of Baudelaire and Hofmannsthal does suggest a kinship between the two poets.

* * *

Let us turn now to some of the works by Hofmannsthal in which the state he later called "Praeexistenz" is expressed. First, an 1896 poem, "Ein Knabe":

I

Lang kannte er die Muscheln nicht für schön,
Er war zu sehr aus einer Welt mit ihnen,
Der Duft der Hyazinthen war ihm nichts
Und nichts das Spiegelbild der eignen Mienen.

Doch alle seine Tage waren so
Geöffnet wie ein leierförmig Tal,
Darin er Herr zugleich und Knecht zugleich
Des weißen Lebens war und ohne Wahl.

Wie einer, der noch tut, was ihm nicht ziemt,
Doch nicht für lange, ging er auf den Wegen:
Der Heimkehr und unendlichem Gespräch
Hob seine Seele ruhig sich entgegen.

II

Eh er gebändigt war für sein Geschick,
Trank er viel Flut, die bitter war und schwer.
Dann richtete er sonderbar sich auf
Und stand am Ufer, seltsam leicht und leer.

Zu seinen Füßen rollten Muscheln hin,
Und Hyazinthen hatte er im Haar,
Und ihre Schönheit wußte er, und auch
Daß dies der Trost des schönen Lebens war.

Doch mit unsicherm Lächeln ließ er sie
Bald wieder fallen, denn ein großer Blick
Auf diese schönen Kerker zeigte ihm
Das eigne unbegreifliche Geschick.

This is not one of Hofmannsthal's greatest poems, but in it the contrast between Praeexistenz and Existenz is stated with unusual clarity. The first three stanzas describe the youth in the first state. The emphasis in the first stanza is on his lack of awareness. Surrounded by the objects of nature, he does not recognize them as beautiful, not out of any insensitivity or indifference, but because he belongs to their world and does not have the detachment required for this aesthetic judgment. This sense is further reinforced by the parallelism of the scent of hyacinths and the mirror reflection of his own countenance; neither is of importance to him. He is in a totally non-reflexive state.

The second stanza goes on to say that all his days are "open" in a way which is compared to a lyre-shaped valley, a strange metaphor which suggests both musical harmony and the fusion of the natural and artificial realms. Geöffnet: here is a suggestion of limitless possibility, further suggested by his dual role of master and servant. And yet this sense of possibility is qualified by his lack of choice. The adjective "weiß" applied to life may suggest purity; but it also has the connotation of a blank slate which has yet to be written on. One is reminded of some of the words Hofmannsthal used to describe this condition in Ad me ipsum: "Geistige Souveränität: sieht die Welt von oben. . . . Nachteil: sieht nur Totalitäten. . . ."[7] In the sense that his life is open and unrestricted, he stands above all and thus is master; but the continuance of this state is contingent on his not making choices, on his remaining on the level of totalities and not "descending" to the level of individual beings; thus his mastery is without real meaning.

The third stanza introduces a slightly jarring note into this harmonious picture: "Wie einer, der noch tut, was ihm nicht ziemt, / Doch nicht für lange. . . ." Here it is suggested that there is something unfitting about this state, and that it cannot in any case last forever: "doch nicht für lange." The note of condemnation is gentle but unmistakable.

If the first section of the poem is a kind of song of innocence, the second is clearly a song of experience. In contrast to the adjective "ruhig" which sums up the first section, his intervening experience, we are told, has been "bitter und schwer." The dialectic of mastery and bondage is carried on in this section, but here it is reversed. Where, before, he appeared to stand above all and yet had no real control, now he has been "gebändigt." But this apparent bondage is in service to his own destiny, in the realm of action where freedom first takes on real meaning. He now knows the beauty of seashells and hyacinths, and knows their importance: "Daß dies der Trost des schönen Lebens war." His consciousness of beauty is tied up with a new self-awareness. Where earlier the hyacinths and his own reflection in the mirror were indifferent to him, he now wears hyacinths in his hair. A final glance at these objects (the _sie_ in the first line of the last stanza seems to refer to both Muscheln and Hyazinthen) reveals them to be "schöne Kerker" which reflect his own destiny. To understand this metaphor we must recall that while the first section is dominated by the idea of openness, here the essential idea is of enclosure. Making choices in life necessarily implies closing off other possibilities. Indeed, the idea of destiny (Geschick) is inseparable from that of necessity and, at least on one level, lack of freedom. Just as the objects are beautiful in spite of (or on account of?) being "prisons," so by accepting this necessity he achieves a mastery which was impossible in the earlier state.

Hofmannsthal's greatest poems tend to be less programmatic than this one, but several do confirm or extend the idea of Praeexistenz derived from "Ein Knabe." In "Die Beiden," the two figures prior to their encounter display a picture of harmony, calm, and apparent mastery. But this mastery does not survive the test of a first encounter: the goblet which she had held so firmly falls to the ground before he can receive it. Thus this lovely poem presents us with an image of the first intrusion of human contact into the lives of individuals in a self-enclosed "pre-existent" state. In "Weltgeheimnis" pre-existence is presented in a more universal and far more positive light:

> Der tiefe Brunen weiß es wohl,
> Einst waren alle tief und stumm,
> Und alle wußten drum.

The <u>es</u> of line 1 and the <u>drum</u> of line 3 clearly refer to the <u>Weltgeheimnis</u> of the title. Here it is suggested that people in the state of <u>Praeexistenz</u> are privy to a secret, some hidden knowledge lost to them later in life, and only recaptured at rare moments, through the experience of love or through an insight into the real content of words, which are described through the metaphor of a piece of gravel holding a precious gem imprisoned inside it. But here, too, the more favorable view of <u>Praeexistenz</u> is balanced by the knowledge that it is a state which cannot last.

There is one work to which we can turn, however, to examine a group of people who are somehow suspended in <u>Praeexistenz</u>: the lyric drama <u>Das kleine Welttheater</u>. In <u>Ad me ipsum</u>, Hofmannsthal says of the figures of this play ". . . jeder dieser Glücklichen irgendwie noch Angehöriger der höchsten Welt, am vollsten teilhaftig der Wahnsinnige."[8] A closer look at two of these figures will serve to extend our picture of <u>Praexistenz</u>.

The poet, the first of these figures, strikes a pose at the beginning which is typical of <u>Praexistenz</u>:

> Nun schreit ich auf und ab den schmalen Pfad,
> Von weitem einem Vogelsteller gleichend,
> Vielmehr dem Wächter, der auf hoher Klippe
> Von ungeheuren Schwärmen großer Fische

>   Den ungewissen Schatten sucht im Meer:
>   Denn über Hügel, über Auen hin
>   Späh ich nach ungewissen Schatten aus. . . .⁹

We recall Hofmannsthal's words from Ad me ipsum, "Geistige Souveränität: sieht die Welt von oben." The poet, surveying the scene below, vaguely senses some ties to the things he sees, tries to penetrate into their mysteries, but never quite succeeds:

>   Gestalten! und sie unterreden sich.
>   O wüßt ich nur, wovon! ein Schicksal ists,
>   und irgendwie bin ich dareinverwebt.¹⁰

His situation is neatly summed up by the words immediately following those quoted above from Ad me ipsum: "Nachteil [of viewing the world from above]: sieht nur Totalitäten."

The figure in whom the state of Praeexistenz is carried out to its most extreme condition is the madman. We meet him first in the extended speech of his servant:

>   Aufgetürmten Schatz an Macht und Schönheit
>   Zehrte er im Tanz wie eine Flamme.
>   Von den Händen flossen ihm die Schätze,
>   Von den Lippen Trunkenheit des Siegers. . . .
>   Und der Vater, der die Flüsse nötigt,
>   Auszuweichen den Zitronengärten . . .
>   Nicht vermag er, seinen Sohn zu bändigen.¹¹

He is described almost as a force of nature which cannot be restrained. The verb bändigen reminds us of the line from "Ein Knabe": "Eh er gebändigt war für sein Geschick." Unlike the youth, who submits to the painful transition into Existenz from his initial state, the madman cannot be tamed and remains in his pre-existent condition. The motif of squandering inherited wealth is reminiscent of the Erbe in the poem "Lebenslied," another example of the totally "open," unrestricted state of limitless possibility we found in the first section of "Ein Knabe." For the madman, who aspires to see into the "Kern," the essence of all being, everything material is a "Schale" to be cast away:

>   Was aber sind Paläste und die Gedichte:
>   Traumhaftes Abbild des Wirklichen!
>   Das Wirkliche fängt kein Gewebe ein. . . .[12]

At the end of the play he tries to jump into the river in an effort to escape the last Schale, his own bodily existence, but is restrained by his attendants. There is of course an admirably quixotic quality to this search for the absolute, but the ending clearly demonstrates that the only consistent result is a complete rejection of normal human existence. For this Existenz, achieved by the youth in the second section of "Ein Knabe," is dependent on an at least provisional acceptance of these "Schalen" as the substance of human life. If it is given to one in the state of Praeexistenz to see through and beyond external façades, it is required of one in Existenz to accept these and the limitations they symbolize in order to lead a social existence in a human community.

* * *

Although the concept of an earlier existence where the individual self is in a state of harmony with the world does not emerge clearly in Mallarmé's mature poetry, it is interesting to note that Jean-Pierre Richard, author of one of the finest studies of Mallarmé, speaks of the poetry of Mallarmé's youth under the rubric of "L'Epoque Séraphique." He has this to say:

> Entre terre et ciel point ici de distance ni d'obstacle. Notre monde est infusé d'être: ou plutôt il se baigne directement dans l'être, se berce en lui, se laisse de toutes parts effleurer, traverser par lui. L'âme enfantine se découvre ainsi délicieusement poreuse: elle vit en contact immédiat et permanent avec une réalité spirituelle qui tout à la fois la comble et la soutient. . . . Dans cet éden d'azur continu, où n'existent ni distance entre les êtres ni obstacle entre les objets, les divers moments de la durée ne se séparent pas non plus les uns des autres. Point encorce ici de différence entre l'avant et l'après, le rêve et l'accompli, l'existence réelle ne fait qu'un avec l'existence virtuelle.[13]

This is an uncannily accurate description of the states we have seen described in Baudelaire and Hofmannsthal, with one important difference. Where the latter two poets wrote their poems as it were retrospectively, having already made the transition into <u>Existenz</u>, Mallarmé's early verse, according to Richard, is written by one still in the earlier state. From this follows a further distinction. In Baudelaire and Hofmannsthal we are never unaware of the fact that this state is limited, both in time and in its apparent perfection. This is indicated in Baudelaire by the past tense of "La Vie Antérieure" and by the "secret douloureux" which calls the rest of the poem into question. In Hofmannsthal it is shown by its juxtaposition with the state of <u>Existenz</u> in "Ein Knabe" and other works, and by showing, through the figure of the madman, the destructive consequences of remaining in this state. In Mallarmé's early verse there can be no such critical detachment since it is, to borrow Hofmannsthal's terminology, the poetry of <u>Praeexistenz</u>, and not of someone reflecting back upon it.

Richard's descriptive phrase "un éden d'azur continu" summons up vividly the ambiance of Baudelaire's poem, and suggests what is perhaps the most substantial survival of this concept in Mallarmé's mature verse: in the motif of <u>l'azur</u>, the symbol of the unattainable ideal which haunts so many figures in Mallarmé, most unforgettably the poet in the poem "L'Azur." Another survival of the concept in his later verse is in the motif of virginity and self-enclosure which runs throughout Mallarmé and is embodied most notably in the figure of Hérodiade. Richard speaks of the breakdown of Mallarmé's "seraphic epoch":

> Or cette unité . . . sera bientôt perdue: la rêverie mallarméenne se divisera alors entre deux besoins contradictoires, elle se déchirera entre le goût de l'inaccompli, de l'envellopé, du vierge, et le désir non moins violent d'actualiser cette virginité, de la manifester en dehors d'elle, de la faire exister dans une durée et dans une monde, de la rendre vivace.

> Mais la vivacité pourra-t-elle se dire encore vierge? Comment vivre à la fois en un deçà et un au delà, comment concilier possible et réel, jaillissement et retenue, silence et parole?[14]

This passage will strike a familiar note with anyone acquainted with Hofmannsthal's works, and particularly as interpreted in <u>Ad me ipsum</u>. When Hofmannsthal speaks of "der ambivalente Zustand zwischen Praeexistenz und Leben,"[15] he is referring to essentially the same conflict, if not always in the same terms. For people in this state, pre-existential harmony has been irretrievably broken, but they still have not drawn the consequences from this and seek to recapture the earlier state. This is the situation <u>par excellence</u> of the aesthete, vividly portrayed in Hofmannsthal's lyrical drama <u>Der Tor und der Tod</u> in the figure of Claudio. Virginity maintained beyond its appropriate time becomes sterility, and this forms the core of Hofmannsthal's critique of aestheticism, which we will examine in the second chapter. Similarly, it is precisely in the dichotomy of virginity/sterility and human fertility where the contrast lies between Hofmannsthal and Mallarmé, which will be developed in the final chapter.

* * *

In reviewing what we have learned in this section, it must be emphasized that the primary concern was not to prove a definite or direct influence of the French poets on the Austrian. In the case of Mallarmé's early verse this would be clearly impossible, since most of this verse was published after the deaths of both poets. In the case of Baudelaire, on the other hand, an influence is not only possible but extremely likely. It is virtually certain that Hofmannsthal had read through and was familiar with the poems of <u>Les Fleurs du Mal</u>, at the latest following his meetings with George in 1891, probably even earlier, and "La Vie Antèrieure" appeared in all editions of <u>Les Fleurs du Mal</u>. Thus the motif of a former harmonious existence was familiar to him through Baudelaire prior to the writing of almost all the major poems and dramas of his "lyrical decade," and prior to the first appearance of Hearn's <u>Kokoro</u> in 1896. Nevertheless, what is important here is not the influence but rather the existence of a topos of remarkable similarity in the three poets, a similarity which is all the more remarkable if one assumes there was <u>no</u> influence. It is difficult to find any precedent for this in earlier literature. To be sure, the topos of a golden age of mankind is nothing new in Western literature; no poet in the German language could be unaffected by the idealization of Greece in these terms as initiated by Winckelmann, Schiller, and Hölderlin.[16] Similarly, the innocent bliss of childhood is a recurrent motif in all literatures. It may well be true, as Schiller once said, that

> . . . jeder Mensch hat sein Paradies, sein goldenes Alter, dessen er sich, je nachdem er mehr oder weniger Poetisches in seiner Natur hat, mit mehr oder weniger Begeisterung erinnert.[17]

But in general this nostalgia has been either expressed as a longing to return to one's own childhood, or projected onto a supposed historical age of mankind. Here, though, we are dealing with something quite different: neither a clearly defined epoch in the history of mankind, nor a specific period in the life of every individual. All that can be said to place this state temporally in Hofmannsthal and Baudelaire is that it is "antérieure," at some time previous to mature human existence. Thus we have located a substantial affinity between Hofmannsthal and two of the major French Symbolists, one which probably would justify a claim of direct influence, and certainly does justify viewing Hofmannsthal in relation to his French predecessors.

Section Two: "Sprachskepsis und Sprachmagie"

In a European context, the name of Hofmannsthal is associated above all with the crisis of language around the turn of the century, a crisis which found its classic expression in "Ein Brief," the famous letter of Lord Chandos which Hofmannsthal wrote in 1902. However, as anyone familiar with his works will testify, Hofmannsthal's meditations on and his problematical relationship with language constitute an element conspicuously present in his writings from the very beginning. They are also an element which ties him to the French Symbolists, above all Mallarmé. To be sure, a radical scepticism concerning language afflicted many writers around the turn of the century, including some outside the Symbolist tradition, such as Gerhart Hauptmann, a writer associated with Naturalism.[18] And yet, as we shall see, there is such a close parallel in the specific terms in which Mallarmé and Hofmannsthal deal with the problem of language that one cannot avoid citing this as one of the chief affinities between the two poets.[19]

The development of this theme will come in two stages. First, in the brief section which follows, I will show a striking parallel between Mallarmé's view of language and that of young Hofmannsthal. Then in the second chapter, particularly in its final section, I will show how this view of language is developed but never fundamentally altered in his later years.

*   *   *

Mallarmé's reflections on language, though based on and in turn influencing his poetic practice, are to be found primarily among his essays published in the volume <u>Divagations</u>. In the essay "Crise de vers" he writes:

> Les langues imparfaites en cela que plusieurs, manque la suprême: penser étant écrire sans accessoires, ni chuchotement mais tacite encore l'immortelle parole, la diversité, sur terre, des idiomes empêche personne de proférer les mots qui, sinon se trouveraient, par une frappe unique, elle-même matériellement la vérité.

There is an opposition here between the diversity of worldly languages, all of them imperfect and debased, and the notion of an ideal utterance, "l'immortelle parole," which would transcend all actual languages and embody the truth materially and directly. He goes on to say:

> . . . tourné à de l'esthétique, mon sens regrette que le discours défaille à exprimer les objets par des touches y répondant en coloris ou en allure, lesquelles existent dans l'instrument de la voix, parmi les langages et quelquefois ches un.[21]

As an example, he points to the annoying fact that the word jour has a dark tone, while nuit is light.

Clearly, this represents a radical critique of language as it is normally used and conceived, i.e., as an arbitrarily given word representing some specific object, thing, or idea in nature. Not only this language, but even the objects thus represented, are viewed with disfavor. Mallarmé claims that the various literary schools current in Paris in the 1880s and 1890s were united in

> . . . un Idéalisme qui . . . refuse les matériaux naturels et, comme brutale, une pensée exacte les ordonnant; pour ne garder de rien que la suggestion.[22]

Thus nature is devalued, along with that use of language which specifies natural objects in a one-to-one relationship; in contrast, language is exalted in its capacity for suggestion. It is not only that language in this sense is suggestive or connotative rather than denotative; it is actually seen as autonomous. Having liberated itself from any specific object of reference, it liberates itself in turn from the writer who "uses" it:

> L'oeuvre pure implique la disparition élocutoire du poëte, qui cède l'initiative aux mots, par le heurt de leur inégalité mobilisés: ils s'allument de reflets réciproques comme une virtuelle traînée de feux sur des pierreries, remplaçant la respiration perceptible en l'ancien souffle lyrique ou la direction personnelle enthousiaste de la phrase.[23]

This new kind of language is opposed on the one hand to the strictly denotative use of words, and on the other to language as a vehicle for personal lyrical effusions. Language has become self-reflexive, free of both subject and object.

The famous passage towards the end of this essay suggests how this language would operate:

> A quoi bon la merveille de transposer un fait de nature en sa presque disparition vibratoire selon le jeu de la parole, cependant; si ce n'est pour qu'en émane, sans la gêne d'un proche ou concret rappel, la notion pure.
> Je dis: une fleur! et, hors de l'oubli où ma voix relègue aucun contour, en tant que quelque chose d'autre que les calices sus, musicalement se lève, idée même et suave, l'absente de tous bouquets. . . .
> Le verse qui de plusieurs vocables refait un mot total, neuf, étranger à la langue et comme incantatoire, achève cet isolement de la parole: niant, d'un trait souverain, le hasard demeuré aux termes malgré l'artifice de leur retrempe alternée en le sens et la sonorité, et vous cause cette surprise, de n'avoir ouï jamais tel fragment ordinaire d'élocution, en même temps que la réminiscence de l'objet nommé baigne dans une neuve atmosphère.[24]

The concept of "la notion pure" and the "absente de tous

bouquets" evoked by the word "fleur" remind one of the Platonic theory of Ideal Forms. But there is an important difference. In Platonic theory the word "flower" evokes the ideal essence <u>common</u> to all actual flowers, but in Mallarmé's "notion pure," all actual flowers disappear to reveal an absence, and all that remains is the word itself, elevated to the level of ultimate reality. The goal of verse is to achieve this "mot total, neuf, étranger à la langue et comme incantatoire."

And yet, though this magical conception of language remains the ideal, Mallarmé is still well aware of the disparity between this and language as it is ordinarily used:

> Un désir indéniable à mon temps est de séparer comme en vue d'attributions différentes le double état de la parole, brut ou immédiat ici, là essentiel.[25]

"Brut ou immédiat" versus "essentiel": the young Hofmannsthal was well aware of this dual nature of language. Consider, for example, these lines from his 1890 Ghasel "Für mich": "Das Wort, das Andern Scheidemünze ist, / Mir ists der Bilderquell, der flimmernd reiche."[26] This is an image which recurs repeatedly in Hofmannsthal's writings. Language, which for most people has been debased to a medium of exchange, a coin, is in the poet's hands an inexhaustible source of images. In the lyric drama <u>Gestern</u>, composed in the same year, the poet Fantasio describes his impression of a procession of flagellants in this way:

> Mir ist, als hätt ich Heiliges erlebt.
> Grad wie wenn Worte, die wir täglich sprechen,
> In unsre Seele plötzlich leuchtend brechen,
> Wenn sich von ihnen das Gemeine hebt
> Und uns ihr Sinn lebendig, ganz erwacht![27]

Though he speaks of language here in analogy to what he has experienced outside, it is clear that this is the same opposition between language as a medium of daily exchange and as a container of an ideal, living meaning. When Fantasio goes on to say: "Wir wandeln stets auf Perlen, staubbedeckt, / Bis ihren Glanz des Zufalls Strahl erweckt,"[28] it is clear that the same conception has been extended in a further image, that of language as a precious stone which is obscured by an exterior coating of dust.

Though these references to language are used in analogy to a separate experience, they also serve, as Peter Szondi has pointed out,[29] to distinguish the poet and real artist Fantasio, who is capable of seeing through to the real essence of words, from the aesthete Andreas, whose response to Fantasio's speech makes it clear that he only understands the literal level of language and applies it directly to his immediate concerns.

The image of the word as a jewel, the value of which is obscured by an outer layer, appears most prominently in the poem "Weltgeheimnis":

> In unsern Worten liegt es drin,
> So tritt des Bettlers Fuß den Kies,
> Der eines Edelsteins Verlies.[30]

Karl Pestalozzi, in his study of <u>Sprachskepsis und Sprachmagie im Werk des jungen Hofmannsthals</u>, the work which introduced these two highly useful terms into general parlance, makes the following comment on the use of <u>es</u> to designate the "Weltgeheimnis" of the poem: "Als das leerste aller Worte vermag es noch am ehesten, die Allheit jenseits aller Dinge zu fassen."[31] Thus in using this word Hofmannsthal illustrates in a striking fashion how the most apparently mundane word can represent the deepest reality. Pestalozzi goes on to say, somewhat later on:

> Wo jedoch die Sprache nicht mehr "in den Grund," das heißt symbolisch begriffen wird, wo die Worte nicht mehr aus der Seelentiefe aussteigen, ist ihr lebendiger Sinn verborgen gleich dem Edelstein im Kies.[32]

This dichotomy appears in Hofmannsthal's essays as well. In "Eine Monographie," an essay on the art of the actor Friedrich Mitterwurzer, a general sense of the inadequacy of words as a means of expression is opposed to Mitterwurzer's performance:

> In seinem Mund werden die Worte auf einmal wieder etwas ganz Elementares, der letzte eindringlichste Ausdruck des Leibes, . . . reine sinnliche Offenbarungen des inneren Zustandes. . . .[33]

Thus we see in Hofmannsthal the same double vision of language we saw in Mallarmé: language as the debased medium of everyday exchange, but also language as the bearer of supreme truth. In this case, it would be difficult to claim a direct influence; as we have seen, this concept appears in Hofmannsthal's work as early as 1890, the year before he met George. While it is conceivable that he was familiar with some of Mallarmé's poetry before this time, it is highly unlikely that he had read any of the essays. Prior to their inclusion in the 1897 volume <u>Divagations</u>, they had appeared only in various Parisian journals. Thus Hofmannsthal almost certainly had his first exposure to Mallarmé's critical theory when George told him about the Tuesday night meetings at Mallarmé's apartment, in which the master would hold forth on his views in terms which are thought to be similar to those of the essays in <u>Divagations</u>. Rather than speaking of influence here, it would be more accurate to describe Hofmannsthal's first encounter with Mallarmé's theory of language in his words from the letter to Walther Brecht: "die Bestätigung dessen, was in mir lag."[34]

This is not to suggest that the two poets defined the dual nature of language in precisely the same terms. Where Mallarmé's supreme Word creates an absence of all natural objects only to become itself the ultimate reality, the higher form of language for Hofmannsthal is the vehicle of ultimate truth, but only its vehicle; the word in and of itself is not raised to an ultimate status as it is in Mallarmé. When, in the essay on Mitterwurzer, Hofmannsthal reports that "die Worte haben sich vor die Dinge gestellt,"[35] he seems to echo Mallarmé, except that it is clear from the context that Hofmannsthal intends this as a negative judgment. Where Mallarmé excluded organic nature from his ideal language, the highest compliment Hofmannsthal could pay to a language was to say that it was <u>living</u> (lebendig). This distinction is clear from the beginning, and has consequences the importance of which increase during the course of Hofmannsthal's career, as we shall see in the chapters which follow.

Section Three: A New Kind of Poetry

In <u>Grundbegriffe der Poetik</u>, the Swiss phenomenological critic Emil Staiger attempted to describe the "essences" of the three major literary modes: lyric, epic, and dramatic. While discussing the nature of the lyric, and in reference to Goethe's "Wanderers Nachtlied," Staiger makes the following comments:

> Im lyrischen Stil . . . wird nicht ein Vorgang sprachlich "wieder"-gegeben. Es ist nicht so, daß in "Wanderers Nachtlied" hier die Abendstimmung wäre, und dort die Sprache mit ihren Lauten zur Verfügung stünde und auf den Gegenstand angewandt würde. Sondern der Abend erklingt als Sprache, von selber; der Dichter "leistet" nichts. Es gibt hier noch kein Gegenüber.[36]

Somewhat later he speaks, in a similar vein, of

> . . . der heikle Begriff der Form, der, wie man
> ihn auch wenden mag, doch immer ein zu Formendes und eine formende Kraft oder eine Art Hohlform, mit der geformt wird, voraussetzt. Eben
> dieses Gegenüber einer Form und eines zu formenden öffnet in lyrischer Dichtung sich
> nicht.[37]

The essence of the lyrical would seem to consist in its lack of any sense of detachment. A situation is not reproduced (wiedergegeben) as in drama or in narrative, but by an almost magical process the subject of the poem "erklingt als Sprache," is transformed directly into the language of the poem. (The ambiguity of the word "subject" here is intentional, for the statement holds true for both the topic or theme and the poetic self of the poem.) The concept of the poem as "spoken" by a dramatic speaker distinct from the poet is clearly ruled out here. The implications of this for a model of poetic creation are made clear in the second quotation. The poet is not regarded as a craftsman carefully shaping and reworking his verbal material, but instead the poem seems to come into being spontaneously.

Let us contrast with Staiger's conception the one reflected in a statement by the American critics Monroe C. Beardsley and W. K. Wimsatt in their famous essay on the "Intentional Fallacy":

> . . . even a short lyric poem is dramatic, the response of a speaker (no matter how abstractly conceived) to a situation (no matter how universalized). We ought to impute the thoughts

> and attitudes of the poem immediately to the dramatic <u>speaker</u>, and if to the author at all, only by an act of biographical inference.³⁸

To be sure, Staiger makes it clear that he is not speaking of the lyric poem as a specific literary genre, but only of "the lyrical" as a basic mode which is naturally to be found predominantly in lyric poetry, but which is not exclusive to it; conversely, a specific lyric poem may partake to some degree of the dramatic or epic modes. This alone, however, can hardly account for the difference between Staiger and the American critics, who see a dramatic element inherent in <u>every</u> lyric poem. A more important reason for this difference, and one more relevant to this discussion, is that the critics are basing their statements on different literary traditions: Staiger claims expertise in and draws his examples from German and ancient Greek lyric poetry, whereas Beardsley and Wimsatt are familiar primarily with the Anglo-American tradition and, perhaps to a lesser degree, with that of French poetry. It is this fact, I believe, which goes a long way toward explaining these totally divergent ideas of the lyric poem.³⁹

One need not accept Staiger's statement in its entirety to recognize its broad applicability to much German lyric poetry from Goethe on through the Romantics and the rest of the nineteenth century. It is no accident that Staiger begins his discussion of the lyric with Goethe's "Wanderers Nachtlied," perhaps the most famous example of that strain in Goethe's lyric output which one could describe as expressing the poet's absorption into and oneness with nature. It is this strain, rather than the more "objective" forms of Goethe's later years, which was carried on by Romantics such as Brentano, Eichendorff, and Mörike, and poets of the mid and late nineteenth century such as Droste-Hülshoff, Hebbel, and Meyer, all cited by Staiger. It is no accident that so much of this poetry has been set to music, for the poems themselves correspond to no other genre so much as that of the <u>Lied</u>, a form which has very little parallel in the Anglo-American or French traditions.

By contrast, these traditions have little of the "Innerlichkeit" and musicality of this German strain. And thus almost all major poetry in English and French can be read in the essentially "dramatic" frame suggested by Beardsley and Wimsatt. To illustrate this point, one need only compare the <u>Lieder</u> of Goethe and his Romantic followers with the poetry being written during the same period in England and France. One thinks of the most famous lyrics of the English Romantics: either they are monologues spoken in a carefully defined dramatic setting (e.g., Wordsworth's "Tintern Abbey," Coleridge's "Frost at Midnight"), ballads or other quasi-narrative forms, odes (which by definition are <u>addressed</u> to some person, thing, or idea), or sonnets, which by their very strictness of form and their tightly constructed "argument" (this is true even of some of the most "lyrical" sonnets, such as those of Keats) are far removed from the German tradition described above. The tradition of French poetry until the Parnassiens, including much of Baudelaire, was with few exceptions a highly rhetorical and public one, which in its almost invariable use of the alexandrine was firmly linked with the drama of Racine and Corneille. Of course there are exceptions to this on both sides of the Rhine; but in spite of this the general tendency seems unmistakable.

The rhetorical quality of most French poetry was one of the central points in the Parnassiens', and later the Symbolists', attack on traditional French verse. Verlaine's advice in "L'Art Poétique," "Prends l'éloquence et tords-lui son cou!" summed up the sentiments of an entire poetic generation. Indeed, it is in the work of Verlaine himself that the French lyric makes its closest approach to the German Lied. Not surprisingly, the only French poem cited by Staiger in his discussion of the lyric is Verlaine's famous "Chanson d'Automne."

And yet it would be a mistake to interpret the Parnassien and Symbolist revolt against Romantic rhetoric as a turn towards the German conception of the lyric expressed by Staiger and exemplified in the Lied. The Parnassiens, it must be recalled, strove above all for an objective, "painterly" approach; far from being absorbed into and thus being a direct communicator of nature, the poet here insists on his detachment from the scene he describes in polished poetic form. The

Symbolists, it is true, moved away from this "painterly" model of poetry toward a musical one. But though Verlaine's dictum "De la musique avant toute chose" reflects an aspiration shared by nearly all the Symbolists, this meant different things to different poets. In Verlaine and some of his followers, it did imply a songlike lyricism which often came very close to the German tradition. But in others, such as Mallarmé, it was something quite different. Though often couched in mystical terms, the "musical" nature of poetry is understood by Mallarmé to mean the essentially non-denotative nature of poetic language, its fundamental "otherness" from everyday speech. When the poetic metaphor is thus liberated from one specific reference, it attains a kind of autonomy comparable to that of a musical motif. The word is no longer a simple signifier of some concrete thing or idea; instead it is a highly potent element which includes all of its potential meanings (including historical meanings long since vanished from ordinary speech), its sound, even its appearance on the printed page, and its association with other words in the poem through rhyme, assonance, alliteration, or orthography. Divorced in this way from its simple "dictionary" meaning, it becomes a structural element within the poem. The poem is built on a progression of metaphors, one suggesting and being modified in turn by the next. Thus Mallarmé's poetry is "musical" in an essentially structural sense, not unlike some twentieth-century novels the structures of which are derived from musical forms.⁴⁰

*　*　*

The preceding discussion, though it may have seemed remote from our theme, is essential if we are to deal with the larger question of the overall impact of French Symbolism on Hofmannsthal's work, as opposed to the adoption of an individual topos such as we discussed in the first section. Let us consider the situation of a young poet whose language is German and who is starting to write around 1890. Except for the late Goethe and Hölderlin (whose work, it must be remembered, was relatively unknown until this century), most of the important German verse of the nineteenth century falls into one of two categories. One is the essentially musical, subjective strain which we have discussed. At its best, this poetry attained a musicality in its language which has hardly been equalled before or since; at its worst, it descended to a kind of confessional lyric in which the lack of detachment endorsed by Staiger is carried to its extreme, and regrettable, consequences. In any case, this was a well whose source, by the end of the nineteenth century, was quite apparently running dry. The other main category consists of the poetry of such men as August Graf von Platen, Emanuel Geibel, and the latter's Munich Circle. These poets favored the strict, "classical" forms of Goethe and Schiller: elegies, odes, sonnets, etc. And yet, except for a few poems by Platen, one looks in vain in the work of these poets for any sign of a strong, original poetic voice; the verdict of literary historians in calling these poets "Epigonen" seems justified.

Thus it was natural that young German and Austrian poets starting out in the 1890s should look abroad for new models. And in France they found a poetic movement whose ideals and aspirations reflected their own, whose masters Baudelaire, Verlaine, and Mallarmé had produced and (in the case of the latter two) were still producing poetry of a quality unknown in the German language for almost half a century. We have already seen how Stefan George introduced Hofmannsthal to the work of these French poets; he did the same for Hofmannsthal's Viennese friend Leopold Andrian and the German poets in George's circle centered around the periodical <u>Blätter für die Kunst</u>. Ten years later, Rainer Maria Rilke from Prague was in Paris as secretary to the sculptor Rodin, and had the opportunity to observe directly the new currents in the Parisian literary and artistic community. Thus it is no exaggeration to speak of a "renouveau poétique d'Allemagne" under the influence of the French movement.[41]

In the remainder of this chapter, two major aspects of Hofmannsthal's absorption of Symbolist theory and practice will be discussed, both closely related to the basic polarity outlined here between the nineteenth-century German musical-subjective lyric and the Anglo-French formal-dramatic conception of the lyric.

A. "Die festen romanischen Formen"

Previous attempts to demonstrate the influence of Symbolism on Hofmannsthal have dealt largely with the echoes of Verlaine in his poetry, both in terms of individual motifs and generally in terms of tone and mood. This is not surprising, because on the face of it, the "mood" of Hofmannsthal's poetry -- the melancholy <u>Weltmüdigkeit</u> of "Ballade des äußeren Lebens," the "Terzinen," and several others -- resembles that of Verlaine more than that of any other Symbolist. Thus critics have compared Verlaine's "Chanson d'Automne" with Hofmannsthal's "Vorfrühling," "Il pleure dans mon coeur" with "Regen in der Dämmerung," and "Clair de Lune" with "Dein Antlitz,"[42] and the echoes of the French poet in Hofmannsthal seem indisputable. And yet if one considers the nature of Verlaine's poetry -- its evocation of evanescence and fragility, the sense of constant motion and change -- it becomes clear that Verlaine's influence took the form essentially of a reinforcement of Hofmannsthal's "Impressionist" tendencies which the poet absorbed initially from his Viennese milieu and which were present in his writing before his meeting with George. On the other hand, the songlike qualities which make Verlaine almost unique among French poets were nothing new in the German tradition, as we have seen.

Hofmannsthal's admiration and affection for Verlaine is expressed repeatedly in his letters and essays and by his friend Leopold Andrian, who quotes him as saying, half-jokingly, "Dem [Verlaine] mache ich so viel nach, wie ich kann." But there are limits to his endorsement of Verlaine's art. In the 1895 essay on the poetry of Francis Vielé-Griffin, Hofmannsthal speaks of Verlaine as a dangerous and seductive influence on lesser talents. His primary charge against Vielé-Griffin is that the latter's verse mimics the style of Verlaine without any authenticity of its own:

> Wenn man früher in Frankreich kein wirklicher Dichter war, war man ein Rhetor und hielt Antithesen und einen gewissen Schwung für die Legitimation der Verse. Heute ist man journaliste . . . : man hat die sehr gefährliche Gabe, fast alle Dinge, die man nicht fühlt und kaum denkt, raffiniert gut und fast schlagend auszudrücken.[43]

It is interesting to note that Hofmannsthal here voices a preference for even mediocre poetry of the earlier French tradition, with its rhetoric and argumentation, to a musical and subjective lyric lacking in the authenticity of personal experience, a judgment which reflects his generally low opinion of the followers of Verlaine and Mallarmé who are the "Symbolists" in the narrowest historical sense.

In contrast to Verlaine's avoidance of "feste Form," Hofmannsthal himself, in his 1929 letter to Walther Brecht in which he describes the importance of the Symbolists in his poetic development, says that the meeting with George and his subsequent discovery of this new poetry confirmed him in his aspiration to create a German poetry which would rank with the work of the great English poets such as Keats, and on the other hand show a connection "mit den festen romanischen Formen."[44] To be sure, Hofmannsthal probably is referring here in part to specific verse forms such as the Italian terza rima which he used on several occasions. But it seems clear that he means more generally the strictness of form which characterizes the poetry of the Romance languages as a whole, and French poetry in particular. And no French poets carried the pursuit of formal perfection to greater lengths than did Mallarmé and other Symbolists. Thus in this statement Hofmannsthal reveals that the influence of French Symbolist poetry, and especially that of Mallarmé, pushed him in a direction diametrically opposed to the tendency of Verlaine.

But this needs further scrutiny. In the light of Hofmannsthal's surprising tolerance for the rhetorical, argumentative tradition in French verse, it is worth noting that the feature which mars most of Hofmannsthal's minor verse is its programmatic tendency; at its worst, it seems little more than a particular argument set to verse. On the other hand, the musicality (in Verlaine's sense) of his greatest verse has blinded many critics to the fundamentally _intellectual_ nature of this verse; intellectual, not in the sense of the direct presentation of an argument, but in the sense that it invites, even compels, the reader to think over what he has read, and to "create" its meaning in his own mind. One recalls the endless controversy surrounding the meaning of the closing lines from "Ballade des äußeren Lebens" ("Und dennoch sagt der viel, der 'Abend' sagt . . ."). Indeed, there is little unanimity concerning the meaning of almost any of Hofmannsthal's major poems.[45]

Even if it is granted that the cerebral nature of much of Hofmannsthal's verse links it with that of Mallarmé, a poet who at first glance seems to have found little direct echo in the Austrian, this is still not exactly what is meant by "feste Formen." Thus the question arises: what formal aspects of Symbolist poetry had an impact on Hofmannsthal's own work? An answer to this question can only emerge from a comparison of poems written by Hofmannsthal from January 1892 onward with poems written prior to this time.[46]

It has not escaped notice that Hofmannsthal's poetry undergoes a significant transformation around this time, and in fact that only in the poems of 1892 does Hofmannsthal seem to have found his mature poetic voice. This is demonstrated by the fact that of the small group of most frequently published poems contained at the beginning of the <u>Gedichte und lyrische Dramen</u> volume of the Herbert Steiner edition, three are from the year 1892 and none from any earlier year. The earlier poems are generally lacking in imagery; many of them seem little more than arguments set to verse. When metaphors do appear they seem labored, as in these lines from "Was ist die Welt?": "Und jedes Menschen wechselndes Gemüt, / Ein Strahl ists, der aus dieser Sonne bricht." Or they seem to echo cliches from typical German nineteenth-century nature poetry, as in "Sturmnacht" ("Es flüsterte lockend die Wellenschar / Von heißem tiefem Verlangen") or "Blühende Bäume."

One poem which points in a new direction is "Wolken." This poem, a first version of which was written as early as 1890, may have been completed as late as January 1892.[47] Though the commonly-made assertion that Hofmannsthal's poetry, along with much of the literature of fin-de-siècle Vienna, is essentially Impressionist is of questionable validity, this is one poem which does convey a specifically Impressionist sense of evanescence amd motion:

> Wogende Bilder,
> Kaum noch begonnen,
> Wachsen sie wilder,
> Sind sie zerronnen, [. . .]
>
> Ein lautloses Gleiten,
> Ledig der Schwere,
> Durch aller Weiten
> Blauende Leere.

Instead of the pedantic and cliché-ridden elements of much of the early poetry, we have here a fairly effective evocation of the constantly-changing cloud formations. The only attempt to relate this motion to any other level of meaning or reality comes in the third stanza:

> Es schwankt gigantisch
> Im Mondesglanz
> Auf meiner Seele
> Ihr Schattentanz.

But this is a rather clumsy intrusion of the poet as subject into the scene; the relation between external spectacle and inner experience is categorically stated but never characterized more fully.

In contrast, let us now consider the poem "Vorfrühling," one of the first to be written after his crucial meeting with George, and arguably his earliest major poem. Like "Wolken," it too conveys a sense of motion. The opening lines are: "Es läuft der Frühlingswind / Durch kahle Alleen . . ." And yet immediately our attention is shifted away from the motion as such by the lines that follow: "Seltsame Dinge sind / In seinem Wehen." In the following stanzas the poet speaks of some of the "seltsame Dinge" which the wind as it were acquires in the course of its wanderings. Some of these relate entirely to the personal sphere:

> Es hat sich gewiegt
> Wo Weinen war,
> Und hat sich geschmiegt
> In zerrüttetes Haar.

In both the third and the fourth stanzas, personal elements mingle with imagery taken from nature:

> Er schüttelte nieder
> Akazienblüten

> Und kühlte die Glieder,
> Die atmend glühten.
>
> Lippen im Lachen
> Hat er berührt,
> Die weichen und wachen
> Fluren durchspürt.

Imagery of sound is combined with visual imagery:

> Er glitt durch die Flöte
> Als schluchzender Schrei,
> An dämmernder Röte
> Flog er vorbei.

The wind passes through interiors, suggesting an absence of sound and light:

> Er flog mit Schweigen
> Durch flüsternde Zimmer
> Und löschte im Neigen
> Der Ampel Schimmer.

The seventh stanza repeats the first, and the poem concludes:

> Durch die glatten
> Kahlen Alleen
> Treibt sein Wehn
> Blasse Schatten.
>
> Und den Duft,
> Den er gebracht
> Von wo er gekommen
> Seit gestern Nacht.

This poem differs in numerous respects from "Wolken." First of all, there is a sense of mystery, even incantation, created by several elements: the repetition of the first stanza in the seventh, the echoing of the phrase "kahle(n) Alleen" in the eighth stanza, and above all the juxtaposition of disparate and unusual imagery. For if this poem is distinguished generally by a far higher degree of poetic craftsmanship and control, it is marked in particular by its deliberate and effective use of imagery. These images do not remain purely visual; phrases such as "die wachen Fluren" and "flüsternde Zimmer" seem deliberately to block any purely "naturalistic" reading, as would still be possible in the case of "Wolken." Instead, the images in turn suggest comparisons, point beyond themselves; they invite the reader to in a sense complete the meaning of the poem, not by simply being carried forward by the motion (as in "Wolken") but by reflecting, creating connections in his own mind. Here we see how the intellectual quality of Hofmannsthal's verse is reflected in poetic technique. The personal sphere never intrudes directly into the poem, but is suggested in phrases like "zerrüttetes Haar" and "Glieder, / Die atmend glühten." And the sense of the mysterious evoked by the juxtaposition of imagery points to the central "mystery" of the poem: just what *is* this spring wind which seems to incorporate and combine all the disparate elements of life? The answer seems clear, particularly if one is familiar with the essay "Der Dichter und diese Zeit": it is the poet himself who takes all the elements of life into himself and out of them creates a "Welt der Bezüge." Thus the wind, traditionally a metaphor for poetic inspiration, here represents the poet in his function as a creator of metaphor, of connections among the disparate elements in reality. The title, with its suggestion of a coming season of renewal and growth, serves to reinforce this meaning.

Almost all of the aspects of this poem which distinguish it from Hofmannsthal's earlier poetry can be attributed to the influence of Symbolism. The very deliberate craftsmanship, the removal of the poet as subject, are as uncharacteristic of the German nineteenth-century tradition as they are characteristic of French Symbolism. The mysterious, almost incantatory quality will be familiar to readers of Symbolist poetry, as will the use of a phrase (e.g., "kahle Alleen") as a kind of musical leitmotif. But above all it is the central role played by metaphor in the poem that shows its affinity to French Symbolism. Metaphor, rather than being a more or less effective ornament (as in most traditional German nineteenth-century verse) is here liberated from any specific reference point and becomes instead the structuring principle of the whole poem. And it is precisely this metaphoric structure which has been shown to be one of the most characteristic features of French Symbolist poetry.[48]

One could say schematically that the difference between "Wolken" and "Vorfrühling" is essentially the difference between Impressionism and Symbolism. Impressionism, in its insistence on sensory data as the only reality, is essentially the internalization of Naturalism, as has often been noted. Hermann Bahr was among the first to recognize the essential kinship of the two movements, speaking of Impressionism as "subjective Naturalism." More recently, Beverly Jean Gibbs, in an article on "Impressionism as a Literary Movement,"[49] pointed out that Impressionism had its origins in Realism and Naturalism, and that all of these movements are alike in that they deal essentially with objective reality. For the Impressionist, this reality is reflected in the mirror of his sensory impressions, but this does not alter the fact that this objective, physical reality is the basis of his art. But as Ulrich Weisstein points out in an article on Impressonism, this movement is fundamentally different from Symbolism, in that Impressionism takes an essentially negative view of the symbol:

> The symbol, after all, carries with it the suggestion of meaning; and there is nothing the impressionist dreads more than an epistemological interpretation of the sense data he has assembled. In that sense, Verlaine's "Art Poétique" may be called a manifesto of poetic impressionism, whereas the poetry of Baudelaire, Mallarmé, and Valéry is more concerned with the intellectual.[50]

After what has been said in this section, it is clear that Hofmannsthal belongs among the latter group.

And once this distinction is clear, it is also clear that the claim made by one critic,[51] that Hofmannsthal adopted Symbolist techniques while maintaining an Impressionist Weltanschauung, must be rejected. The metaphorical principle used by Hofmannsthal and the Symbolists implies associations among discrete metaphors and images which transcend the merely sensory level. This is related to the doctrine enunciated in Baudelaire's sonnet "Correspondances," which suggests the mingling of disparate sensory data into a "vaste et profonde unité," and also the existence of mysterious connections between inner and outer reality. Thus the form and content cannot so neatly be separated; the metaphorical principle has implications for the content of the poetry. Metaphor, says Hofmannsthal in a passage from the essay "Bildlicher Ausdruck," is "Kern und Wesen aller Poesie" -- hardly the statement of someone who regards it as merely a technique, a poetic device!

Thus Hofmannsthal gained from his study of French Symbolist poetry a much stronger sense of poetic form and craftsmanship, most significantly in his use of metaphor and imagery. But this new sense of form is also clear in the greater objectivity, the avoidance of confessional elements in his poetry from 1892 onward. It has been pointed out that the words Seele and Herz appear in most of Hofmannsthal's early poems, and disappear almost entirely from the ones written after this time. This transformation in his poetry is in many ways parallel to that which is evident in the work of a poet who was Hofmannsthal's contemporary: Rainer Maria Rilke. Working in Paris as secretary to Rodin, Rilke too learned to put aside the subjective excesses that marred much of his early verse in favor of the detached craftsmanship of the Neue Gedichte:

here too the French influence was crucial, though Rilke's chief model was a sculptor rather than a poet.

Thus we have seen how the French Symbolist influence caused Hofmannsthal to break away from the nineteenth-century German tradition, above all in his use of metaphoric structure. This break can also be seen in another aspect of Hofmannsthal's poetic work; and it is to this we shall turn in the section that follows.

B. Dramatic Lyric and Lyrical Drama

In contrast to the non-dramatic view of the lyric espoused by Emil Staiger, Anglo-American critics have tended to view the lyric in essentially dramatic terms. Rather than being the direct expression of the poet's subjectivity, it is spoken by a persona distinct from the poet himself, and in a particular context. To suggest, as I will in this section, that Hofmannsthal's mature poetry tends to conform, to a far greater degree, to this "dramatic" model than do his early poems, is hardly earthshaking. After all, Hofmannsthal's career as a whole might with some justification be characterized as an increasingly single-minded quest toward dramatic form. What may strike some as surprising is that this turn to dramatic form, at least as it manifests itself in his lyric poetry, comes to a large degree as a consequence of his study of French Symbolist writings.

This claim hardly squares with the conventional wisdom

that Hofmannsthal's turn to the drama and his concomitant abandonment of the lyric genre around the turn of the century represented a decisive break with the Symbolist/Aestheticist background of his "lyrical decade." The Symbolists, after all, were notorious for their disdain of all public utterance, for their cultivation of the arcane and the obscure. And yet this is a false picture. Among the major Symbolists, Villiers de l'Isle-Adam, Maurice Maeterlinck and, later on, Paul Claudel were primarily dramatists. Maeterlinck, in fact, is the one Symbolist writer whose influence on Hofmannsthal was recognized at an early date and never seriously disputed.[52] The Belgian dramatist is referred to familiarly in an essay on Maurice Barrès published in 1891 and written prior to the meeting with George; and thus it is most probable that this familiarity predates the writing of Hofmannsthal's first major work, the one-act lyrical drama Gestern, also published in 1891. In 1892 he made a private translation of Maeterlinck's Les Aveugles which has never been published. In 1900 the two men actually met in Paris; and Hofmannsthal's letters to several Viennese friends, written around this time, testify to the strong impression Maeterlinck made on him. Numerous elements in Hofmannsthal's lyrical dramas have been shown to be modelled on Maeterlinck's plays. More generally, Maeterlinck's conception of the drame statique, in which revelation replaces action, and in which the leading figures are portrayed as victims of forces beyond their control, left its mark on almost all of Hofmannsthal's lyrical dramas.

All of this, as pointed out, has been fairly well established in Hofmannsthal criticism. But the fact that Mallarmé himself, apparently the most arcane and private of Symbolist poets, could actually have been a model in terms of <u>dramatic</u> form, has usually escaped notice. As Haskell M. Block points out in his study, <u>Mallarmé and the Symbolist Drama</u>, "any overall view of Mallarmé's development must consider his continuous and intimate affiliation with the theater."[53] One is reminded that his two most famous poems, "Hérodiade" and "L'Après-midi d'un faune," were both conceived originally as dramas and intended for performance at the Théâtre Français. After his friend Théodore de Banville, who was to have helped Mallarmé's works to a performance, made it clear to him that the two works were admirable poems but impossible to perform, he accepted this judgment and revised the works as poems to be read rather than performed, but they still remain essentially dramatic in form: "L'Après-midi d'un faune" is a dramatic monologue spoken by the faun, and the "Scène" from "Hérodiade" (the only part of the work published before 1913) is a dialogue between Hérodiade and her nurse. This suggests that the distinction between lyrical drama and "dramatic" lyric is a difficult, and at times impossible, one to make. Block goes on to say:

> From the beginning of his career, Mallarmé was intensely aware of the dramatic element in

poetry. Of his early poem, "L'Azur," he declared, "il ya a là un vrai drame." . . . he experienced the conflict of the actual and the ideal as an inherently dramatic quality of his poetry.[54]

In addition to "Hérodiade," "L'Après-midi d'un faune," and "L'Azur," numerous other of Mallarmé's poems present an essentially dramatic situation, even if this situation has to be "pieced together" amidst passages of great philosophical and linguistic complexity, as in "Prose (pour Des Esseintes)."

Peter Szondi, in Das lyrische Drama des Fin-de-siècle,[55] suggests that the "Scène" from Mallarmé's "Hérodiade," though it remained a fragment and though Mallarmé, until the end of his life, intended to complete it, became the model for all the lyrical dramas written around the turn of the century, most notably those by Maeterlinck and Hofmannsthal. First published in Le Parnasse Contemporain of 1869 and reprinted in 1886 and 1887, the "Scène" was certainly familiar to Maeterlinck and was undoubtedly among the first poems by Mallarmé that George brought to Hofmannsthal's attention (George was to translate it into German shortly thereafter). Most importantly, no scene could possibly conform more precisely to Maeterlinck's concept of the "drame statique." The crucial event of the legend, the beheading of John the Baptist, never occurs in the work as we have it. Thus the scene consists of the revelation of Hérodiade and her predicament, the nurse's main function being to set off Hérodiade all the more clearly from normal humanity. But stopping short of the main event of the legend, Mallarmé allows his heroine to remain passive, a "victime lamentable à son destin offerte," rather than becoming a victimizer.

What concerns us here, however, is the impact of this "dramatic" quality of much of Mallarmé's poetry on Hofmannsthal's poetry, rather than on his lyrical dramas -- to the extent that one can separate the two. When one considers the function of this turn to dramatic form in the development of each author's poetic style, one is faced with a striking parallel. During his tenure as an English teacher in the provincial city of Tournon in the mid-1860s, Mallarmé underwent a profound spiritual crisis, eloquently described in the letters he wrote during this time, which caused a drastic change in the nature of his poetry. This is the period in which he wrote the "Scène" from "Hérodiade," and it was in the course of composing this work that he developed the unique style and poetic which were to remain essentially the same throughout the rest of his career. Emilie Noulet has written:

> Avec "Hérodiade" [Mallarmé] s'est délivré de lui-même; du poids de son âme; de la fièvre de fierté et de gloire que l'on porte avec soi dans sa jeunesse; élans, mécontentements, ivresses, malaises, souffrances moroses, thèmes anecdotiques de poésie, ce que la rêverie est à la pensée.
> Après "Hérodiade," nulle poésie ne sera plus décantée que la sienne; plus pure de tout élément trouble et sentimental. Plus personelle dans son écriture, plus impersonelle dans son émotion.[56]

It is clear that the choice of dramatic form is crucial to this accomplishment; by incorporating his own haunting sense of nothingness in the figure of the virginal princess, he exorcised his own private demon, thereby universalizing his theme and creating a poetry of great beauty and clarity.

The same is true for Hofmannsthal. We noted in the previous section that much of Hofmannsthal's earliest verse is marred by its uncontrolled subjectivity. The change that occurs in this regard can be seen by comparing the early poem "Frage" with the 1896 poem "Dein Antlitz."[57] Although both are addressed to a lover, there is a world of difference between them. Szondi points out that in the early poem, the question form serves merely to suggest the connection of the speaker to an implied "Du." The apparent dialogue is actually a monologue of a speaker who cannot make any contact with the "Du" because of his own self-involvement. He is similar in this respect to Andrea, the hero of Gestern. But in the play Hofmannsthal succeeds in externalizing this situation in a dramatic character, thus allowing him to present it with critical detachment, whereas the poem achieves no such detachment; the failure of the poem's speaker reflects the failure of the poem, and it is probably justified to relate this to the autobiographical element which Hofmannsthal later acknowledged to exist in his early work. In the second poem, the tension between the speaker's private experience and his experience of the "Du" is made explicit in the form of a vision of his earlier absorption into nature. But here this earlier experience is implicity rejected -- its beauty, we are told, was "unfructbar" -- in favor of the present.

The simplistic dichotomy, maintained by many critics, between the "lyrical" phase of Hofmannsthal's earlier years and the "dramatic" phase of his maturity, has prevented a general recognition of the dramatic aspect of Hofmannsthal's lyric poetry, but there are a few exceptions to this. Hermann Broch, whose study, <u>Hofmannsthal und seine Zeit</u>, despite many questionable assertions, remains one of the most insightful essays on the poet and on the artistic and intellectual climate of Vienna around the turn of the century, has this to say:

> [Hofmannsthals] frühe Wendung zur Kunst und zur Dichtung entpuppt sich von Anfang an schier eindeutig als Wendung zum Theater, als eine so radikale Wendung, daß sie sogar das lyrische Gedicht auf eine imaginäre Bühnenszene versetzt. Mit andern Worten, der Dichter entwikkelt die lyrische Situation nicht von ihrem Kern her, der auch der seine ist, sondern steht ihr und damit sich selber publikumshaft als Betrachter gegenüber.[58]

This is admirably stated; my only objection would be to emphasize once more that this dramatic element was <u>not</u> present in his earliest poems, and that it entered his lyrical work only after his meeting with George. The change that took place as an immediate result of this meeting is documented by Christa Saas in a paper on "Das Sonettproblem bei Hofmannsthal." Referring to the two sonnets "Der Prophet" and "Mein

Garten" which Hofmannsthal wrote immediately after his first encounter with George, she speaks of the new technique the poet uses:

> er setzt eine ordnende Bildfigur in den Mittelpunkt und schafft für sie eine potentiell dramatische Situation und Spannung. . . . Das monologisch-reflexive Sonett, das der früheste Hofmannsthal gepflegt hat, ist also von einem dramatischen, potentiell dialogischen abgelöst worden. . . . Gewiß kann man sagen, daß Hofmannsthal das monologische Element seiner früheren Sonette völlig durch dialogisch-dramatische Situationen ersetzt und bis zur Perfektion gesteigert und kontrolliert hat.[59]

To this I would only add that the reason for this new poetic technique in his sonnets and other lyric poems is his recent introduction to Symbolist poetry.

Let us now examine some of the stages of this externalization in Hofmannsthal's poetry. One of the poems that the poet himself included in all the collections of his poetry published in his lifetime, and one of his finest, is "Erlebnis," written in 1892:

> Mit silbergrauem Dufte war das Tal
> Der Dämmerung erfüllt, wie wenn das Mond
> Durch Wolken sickert. Doch es war nicht Nacht.
> Mit silbergrauem Duft des dunklen Tales
> Verschwammen meine dämmernden Gedanken,
> Und still versank ich in dem webenden,
> Durchsichtigen Meere und verließ das Leben.
> Wie wunderbare Blumen waren da
> Mit Kelchen dunkelglühend! Pflanzendickicht,
> Durch das ein gelbrot Licht wie von Topasen
> In warmen Strömen drang und glomm. Das Ganze
> War angefüllt mit einem tiefen Schwellen
> Schwermütiger Musik. Und dieses wußt ich,
> Obgleich ichs nicht begreife, doch ich wußt es:

>   Das ist der Tod. Der ist Musik geworden,
>   Gewaltig sehnend, süß und dunkelglühend,
>   Verwandt der tiefsten Schwermut.
>
>   Aber seltsam:
>   Ein namenloses Heimweh weinte lautlos
>   In meiner Seele nach dem Leben, weinte,
>   Wie einer weint, wenn er auf großem Seeschiff
>   Mit gelben Riesensegeln gegen Abend
>   Auf dunkelblauem Wasser an der Stadt,
>   Der Vaterstadt, vorüberfährt. Da sieht er
>   Die Gassen, hört die Brunnen rauschen, riecht
>   Den Duft der Fliederbüsche, sieht sich selber,
>   Ein Kind, am Ufer stehen, mit Kindesaugen,
>   Die ängstlich sind und weinen wollen, sieht
>   Durchs offene Fenster Licht in seinem Zimmer--
>   Das große Seeschiff aber trägt ihn weiter
>   Auf dunkelblauem Wasser lautlos gleitend
>   Mit gelben fremdgeformten Riesensegeln.

The poem is a monologue, and is divided into two sections. The first describes an experience of an immersion of the self in nature: "still versank ich in dem webenden, / Durchsichtigen Meere. . . ." But all the rich, tropical imagery cannot conceal from him the real nature of his experience: it is a deathlike state, utterly removed from life. This insight is stated in the first section, but without any pathos. The second section describes the speaker's "Heimweh nach dem Leben," not in emotional terms, but through an image which is one of the most striking in the poet's work. The speaker weeps, as does a man travelling on a ship in the evening who passes by his homeland. What he sees there is a vision of himself as a child standing on the shore with a child's eyes "die ängstlich sind und weinen wollen." But the vision is a brief one, as the fast ship carries him onward through the night.

What has happened here? The speaker of the poem, in his deathlike trance, is shown a vision of himself in a state of innocence, but he cannot seize this vision and is borne onward against his own will; he is hopelessly separated from his own essential self with all its original possibilities. But this separation is conveyed not through direct statement, as it might have been in an earlier poem. The "self" of the poem is actually two selves, one which observes the other. It is this externalization of the second self which lends this poem its power, in contrast to the speaker in "Frage" who is unaware that he sees only his own image in the "Du" of the poem.

In the series of poems entitled "Gestalten," composed in the years from 1895 onward (the 1893 poem "Hirtenknabe singt" is a forerunner of these), this externalization is carried further. Several of these are spoken by a dramatic persona, defined by the title, who is clearly distinct from the poet. Such a poem is "Der Kaiser von China spricht." In the almost ritualistic majesty of its lines the emperor expresses the "Weltbesitz" associated with the state of Praexistenz, but here this possession is quite literal: he surveys the world and sees it as surrounding him in concentric circles, and he is master of all he sees. The poem is a memorable expression of a feeling of total mastery, an expression which is effective principally because it is spoken by a dramatic persona in the measured, hieratic speech befitting him, rather than being a direct expression of youthful delusions of grandeur.

"Idylle," written in 1893, is in effect a lyrical drama, though it is included among the poems in the Herbert Steiner edition. As has been pointed out, the distinction is often hard to make and is perhaps unnecessary. In this work, an ambivalence in the poet himself is represented in the contrasting figures of the blacksmith and his wife. The woman dreamily recalls her father at work at his potter's craft, visualizing the mythological images he created which to her are a "mahnendes Gedenken andern Lebens," of a life, that is, other than the relatively prosaic world and craft of her husband. He reprimands her and urges her to regard as holy his handiwork, "Das aus des mütterlichen Grundes Eingeweiden stammt." The couple is visited by a centaur, who commissions the smith to make him a new spear point. As the smith works, the centaur regales the wife with lyrical accounts of naiads, satyrs, and even the flute music of the god Pan. This is the world she has dreamed of, and when he turns to leave, she resolves to go with him. But as she departs on the centaur's back, the smith catches sight of them and kills her with a cast of his spear. It is this final tableau of the centaur with a wounded woman by a river's edge which was on the Greek vase which inspired the poem.

One misses the whole point of the work if one identifies either the smith or his wife as representing exclusively Hofmannsthal's own point of view, as some critics have done. A case could be made for either view. The wife's impatience with her husband's craft is echoed by the youthful poet in his 1890 poem "Gedankenspuk": "Wir tragen im Innern / Leuchtend die Charis, / Die strahlende Ahnung der Kunst. / Aber die Götter haben sie tückisch / Mit dem Hephästos vermählt: / Dem schmierigen Handwerk. . . ." On the other hand, the smith's defense of his honest craft, his insistence on the virtues of reverence and the observance of the proper limits to human existence are in harmony with the views of the mature poet, and essentially the same traits are portrayed with evident sympathy in the figure of Barak in Die Frau ohne Schatten. In spite of his sympathy with the woman and her longings, Hofmannsthal portrays her situation clearly as the failure to accept one's adult existence, and the retreat into a dream world (or in the language of Ad me ipsum, an attempt to linger in a pre-existent state), and he shows the disastrous consequences stemming from the confrontation of a person in this state with the pitiless forces of reality. Thus although the smith's point of view emerges as the more appropriate one, this is not accomplished by endorsing the smith's heavy-handed moral condemnation of his wife, but by presenting the consequences of her attitude in dramatic form. At the same time, this form enables the poet to present the woman's feelings sympathetically and in depth, which serves to increase the poignancy of the ending. In the detachment allowed by dramatic form, the poet is able to control his own ambivalence and thus to express it successfully in artistic form.

The long speech of Gianino from <u>Der Tod des Tizian</u> which begins "Mir wars, als ginge durch die blaue Nacht . . .," though part of a lyrical drama, is also one of the poet's most nearly perfect lyrics, and has been treated as such by several commentators. In it, the youth describes a nocturnal vision of Life (the capital letter is obligatory here) at its most intense and vivid, a vision which encompasses nature and imaginative reality, as well as the life of men in the city below. As such, it is a poem which stands by itself and which can with some justification be discussed out of context. And yet it acquires an added meaning from its dramatic context, for Gianino and his vision are juxtaposed with the older disciples of Tizian who can no longer have such visions, who separate themselves from life in the city below in bitter hostility mixed with fear, and who live only vicariously through the master's work. Though the pre-existent state of the youth is presented, at least on the face of it, in a highly favorable light, the failure of his older colleagues is a hint that this visionary anticipation cannot survive a confrontation with the ugliness of the real world. Once again, the dramatic context qualifies and defines the lyrical expression.

If the study of Symbolist writings led Hofmannsthal to adopt dramatic form in his poetry, it also had the complementary effect of strengthening the lyrical element in his lyrical dramas, a fact which becomes apparent if one compares

Gestern, the only lyrical drama written prior to the meeting with George, with those that follow. Examining the works he wrote in 1890 and 1891, one notes the sharp contrast between, on the one hand, the uncontrolled subjectivity of many of the poems, and on the other, the cold, analytical detachment of Gestern. It is this quality of detachment, achieved through dramatic form, which accounts for the relative artistic success of the play. And yet there is something almost too neat, almost mechanical, in the way Andrea's hedonistic, aestheticist Lebensprogramm is refuted by the course of events. The longer speeches of Andrea, such as his praise of sin and mendacity, are all programmatic, and have none of the lyrical intensity, the immersion in the individual character, which mark the speech of Gianino, those of the smith's wife, or those of Claudio in Der Tor und der Tod. The portrait of Andrea is totally unsympathetic and ultimately flat, and thus we are unmoved by the ending of the play.

In sum, what Hofmannsthal learned from the French Symbolists was to combine lyrical and dramatic form in such a way as to lend a greater depth and intensity to the figures and Weltanschauungen portrayed in his dramatic works, while at the same time lending a critical detachment and objectivity to his lyrical expression.

In this turn to dramatic form, as well as in the adoption of the metaphor as a structural principle in his poetry, Hofmannsthal makes a decisive move away from the Innerlichkeit of the German lyric of the nineteenth century and seeks externalization above all. Where Novalis had proclaimed, "Nach innen geht der geheimnisvolle Weg," Hofmannsthal, as if in reply, insists: "Wollen wir uns finden, so dürfen wir nicht in unser Inneres hinabsteigen: draußen sind wir zu finden, draußen." It is no accident that these words should appear in the <u>Gespräch über Gedichte</u>, the fictional dialogue in which Hofmannsthal makes what is perhaps his most explicit affirmation of Symbolist aesthetics. For as we have seen, it was the example of French Symbolism which led Hofmannsthal away from German <u>Innerlichkeit</u> towards a poetry of <u>externality</u>.

*   *   *

In this chapter we have attempted to locate several points of similarity which connect Hofmannsthal with the French symbolist poets, particularly Baudelaire and Mallarmé. In doing so, it has not always been possible to distinguish clearly between actual influence and "accidental" affinities, nor does such a distinction seem crucial to our argument. Even more than the areas of direct influence, it is these striking affinities preceding any direct contact which provide a justification for regarding Hofmannsthal as part of a <u>European</u> Symbolist movement which extends far beyond the cultural boundaries of France. Perhaps no one has put it better than Hofmannsthal himself in his 1929 letter to Walther Brecht, when he speaks of the meeting with George and his discovery of

Symbolist literature: "Im Ganzen kann man sagen, daß die Begegnung von entscheidender Bedeutung war -- die Bestätigung dessen, was in mir lag, die Bekräftigung, daß ich kein ganz vereinzelter Sonderling war. . . ."[60] All creative influence is in a sense a confirmation and strengthening of what one already possesses, and thus it makes no sense to deny the Symbolist influence on Hofmannsthal by pointing to "Symbolist" elements in his work prior to his acquaintance with Symbolist writings. But it is equally wide of the mark to minimize the importance of these poets for Hofmannsthal by showing the great differences that exist between him and individual Symbolists, as have some critics.[61] It goes without saying that whatever Hofmannsthal adopted from other writers he made into something all his own. This is true of his adapatations of Greek tragedy, English medieval morality plays, and Spanish Golden Age theater; and it is no less true of his relation to the Symbolists. Much as his writing may have been transformed through his discovery of the French Symbolists, he was to go his own way as an artist, a path we will trace in the chapters which follow.

Notes

[1] First appeared in <u>Jahrbuch des Freien Deutschen Hochstifts</u> (Frankfurt am Main: E. Brügel & Sohn, 1930), pp. 322-331, later in <u>A</u>, pp. 211-245.

[2] <u>A</u>, p. 21.

[3] <u>A</u>, p. 21.

[4] <u>A</u>, p. 21.

[5] Werner Metzeler, <u>Ursprung und Krise von Hofmannsthals Mystik</u> (Munich: Bergstadt Verlag, 1956), pp. 50-51; Ellen Ritter, "Über den Begriff Praeexistenz bei Hugo von Hofmannsthal," <u>Germanisch-Romanische Monatsschrift</u>, 12, No. 2 (1972), 197-200.

[6] <u>A</u>, p. 213.

[7] <u>A</u>, p. 213.

[8] <u>A</u>, p. 215.

[9] <u>GLD</u>, pp. 297-98.

[10] <u>GLD</u>, pp. 298.

[11] <u>GLD</u>, pp. 309.

[12] <u>GLD</u>, pp. 316.

[13] Jean-Pierre Richard, <u>L'univers imaginaire de Mallarmé</u> (Paris: Editions du Seuil, 1961), pp. 41-43.

[14] Richard, p. 43.

[15] <u>A</u>, p. 216.

[16] For a discussion of this theme in German literature, see Julius Petersen, <u>Die Sehnuscht nach dem dritten Reich in deutscher Sage und Dichtung</u> (Stuttgart: J. B. Metzler, 1934).

[17] Quoted in Petersen, pp. 5-6.

[18] See Theodore Ziolkowski, "Gerhart Hauptmann and the Problem of Language," <u>Germanic Review</u>, 37, No. 4 (1963), 295-306.

[19] My treatment of this question differs significantly from that of Richard Brinkmann in his classic essay on "Hofmannsthal und die Sprache" (<u>Deutsche Vierteljahrsschrift</u>, 35, No. 1 [1961], 69-95). To begin with, the examples I will cite in this section are all taken from Hofmannsthal's works in the 1890s, whereas Brinkmann's essay is concerned primarily with the poet's resolution of the language problem after 1902, the year of "Ein Brief." In analyzing "Ein Brief," Brinkmann extrapolates from the facts of Hofmannsthal's career to interpret the work as essentially a rejection of the language of lyrical poetry. Though it is true that the poet after this time abandoned lyric poetry almost completely as a medium for his own expression, it is also true that "Ein Brief" makes no reference whatever to lyric poetry, and that what it does describe is a loss of cognition accompanied by the failure of conceptual language, followed by the inability to use language even for simple communication. As I will argue later, the fact that Hofmannsthal did write two of his finest lyrics and the "Gespräch über Gedichte" after this time suggests that Brinkmann's view of "Ein Brief" as a specific rejection of

lyric poetry, a view shared by Hermann Broch and several other critics, needs serious qualification. Brinkmann's great accomplishment is in showing how Hofmannsthal found a solution to the problem of language in his turn to the drama. Though there persists a radical mistrust of words as abstract signifiers, nevertheless words spoken by a dramatic speaker in a given context, accompanied by gestures and pauses (which are considered to be part of language) are able to communicate, since language of this kind is the direct expression of lived experience, not just a concretized and thus no longer living form of past experience. This is a fine insight and, as far as it goes, quite indisputable. But two points need to be made. First of all, it is clear from the terms used above that Hofmannsthal's main antipathy was to the language of abstract concepts, not to poetic language as such; indeed, the final section of this chapter will show that Hofmannsthal was able to make use of the "relational" quality of dramatic language even in his lyric poetry. Secondly, what Brinkmann demonstrates so well is only one aspect of the mature poet's view of language. The radical scepticism of <u>Der Schwierige</u>, where (as Brinkmann shows) language becomes possible only through its own negation, exists alongside the almost religious faith in the powers of language expressed in the essays of Hofmannsthal's final decade. Though it is true that language is conceived in these essays in social terms as the binding force of a nation, this does not imply (as Brinkmann would have us believe) that Hofmannsthal is concerned with language only as it is spoken among individuals in a social setting; one of his final essays specifically singles out Mallarmé and the Symbolists for praise in their struggle to revive the inner life of the French language. Thus it is clear that the poet remained passionately concerned with the language of lyric poetry up to the end of his life.

[20] Stephane Mallarmé, Oeuvres Complètes, ed. Henri Mondor and G. Jean-Aubry (Paris: Gallimard, 1970), pp. 363-64.

[21] Mallarmé, p. 364.

[22] Mallarmé, p. 365.

[23] Mallarmé, p. 366.

[24] Mallarmé, p. 368.

[25] Mallarmé, p. 368.

[26] GLD, p. 471.

[27] GLD, p. 171.

[28] GLD, p. 172.

[29] Peter Szondi, Das lyrische Drama des Fin-de-siècle (Frankfurt: Suhrkamp, 1975), pp. 198-204.

[30] GLD, p. 15.

[31] Karl Pestalozzi, Sprachskepsis und Sprachmagie im Werk des jungen Hofmannsthals (Zürich: Atlantis Verlag, 1958), p. 31.

[32] Pestalozzi, p. 41.

[33] PI, p. 230.

[34] Robert Boehringer, Mein Bild von Stefan George, 2nd

ed. (Munich/Düsseldorf: Helmut Küpper, 1967), p. 227.

[35] PI, p. 228.

[36] Emil Staiger, Grundbegriffe der Poetik (Zürich: Atlantis Verlag, 1946), p. 15.

[37] Staiger, p. 21

[38] Monroe C. Beardsley and W. K. Wimsatt, "The Intentional Fallacy" in W. K. Wimsatt, The Verbal Icon (London: Farrar, Straus & Giroux, 1966), p. 5.

[39] This claim is lent support by René Wellek in his essay on "Genre Theory, the Lyric, and Erlebnis" published in Discriminations: Further Concepts of Criticism (New Haven and London: Yale University Press, 1970). Wellek points out that Staiger's three modes, and particularly his conception of the lyrical, are descended from a long tradition in German aesthetics, and could only be supported by the German "Stimmungsgedichte" which Staiger takes as his examples.

[40] See Theodore Ziolkowski's analysis of "sonata-form" in Steppenwolf in his study of The Novels of Hermann Hesse (Princeton: Princeton University Press, 1965); also Thomas Mann's reference to the "symphonic" form of Der Zauberberg.

[41] Enid Lowrie Duthie, L'Influence du symbolisme français dans le renouveau poétique de l'Allemagne (Paris: Honoré Champion, 1933).

[42] Karl Foldenauer, "Hugo von Hofmannsthal und die französische Literatur des 19. und 20. Jahrhunderts" (Diss. Tübingen 1958); Steven P. Sondrup, Hofmannsthal and the French

Symbolist Tradition (Bern: Herbert Lang, 1976).

[43] PI, p. 222.

[44] Boehringer, p. 227.

[45] Thus Foldenauer is essentially correct when he asserts that "für die französischen Symbolisten und für Hugo von Hofmannsthal ist Poesie in erster Linie Geist, nicht Leidenschaft, Hingerissensein oder Natur." In this connection he quotes from a 1934 dissertaton in which Hofmannsthal is compared unfavorably with Goethe and the German lyric tradition following from him: "Es ist [in Hofmannsthals Gedichten] die den ganzen Menschen erfüllende unmittelbare Leidenschaft selten vorhanden, das naturhafte Hingerissenwerden." (Foldenauer, p. 97) This is of course a simple statement of fact; only from the lips of someone whose conception of the lyric is based on the nineteenth-century German tradition does this become a criticism.

[46] The argument on the following pages parallels that of Hans Steffens in his article "Hofmannsthals Übernahme der symbolistischen Technik," Literatur und Geistesgeschichte (Berlin: Schmidt, 1968), pp. 271-79. I am in essential agreement with Steffens, except for the forced distinction he makes between the Symbolist "technique" which he shows Hofmannsthal to have adopted -- through an analysis of "Einem, der vorübergeht," the poem to Stefan George which Hofmannsthal wrote shortly after their first meeting -- and the Symbolist "Kunstprogramm," which he suggests consists essentially of

decadence, and which Hofmannsthal is said to have rejected in toto.

[47]See Eugene M. Weber, "A Chronology of Hofmannsthal's Poems," Euphorion, 63 (1969), esp. 294-97.

[48]See, for instance, Peter Szondi, Das lyrische Drama des fin-de-siècle (Frankfurt: Suhrkamp, 1975), pp. 115, and Steffens.

[49]Modern Language Journal, 36, No. 4 (1952), 175-83.

[50]Encyclopedia of Poetry and Poetics, ed. Alex Preminger (Princeton: Princeton University Press, 1971), pp. 381ff.

[51]Steffens.

[52]See, for instance, Foldenauer, pp. 157-81 and Michel Vanhelleputte, "Hofmannsthal and Maeterlinck," in Hofmannsthal-Forschungen I (Basel: Hugo von Hofmannsthal-Gesellschaft, 1971).

[53]Mallarmé and the Symbolist Drama (Detroit: Wayne State University Press, 1963), p. 6.

[54]Block, p. 7.

[55]See footnote 48.

[56]L'oeuvre poétique de Stéphane Mallarmé (Paris: E. Droz, 1940), pp. 98f.

[57]See Szondi, p. 273.

[58]Hermann Broch, Dichten und Erkennen. Essays: Band I (Zürich: Rhein, 1955), p. 127.

[59]An unpublished paper delivered at the Hofmannsthal

Special Session of the MLA Convention in December 1976. My thanks to Professor Saas for providing me with a copy of her paper.

[60] Boehringer, p. 227.

[61] e.g., Bernhard Böschenstein, "Hofmannsthal und der europäische Symbolismus" in <u>Hofmannsthal-Forschungen</u> II (Freiburg: Hugo von Hofmannsthal-Gesellschaft, 1974), pp. 73-87.

CHAPTER TWO

THE RECONCILIATION OF POETRY AND LIFE

We have seen in the first chapter the extent to which Hofmannsthal absorbed into his own work various aspects of French Symbolist poetic practice and theory, as well as individual motifs and topoi. But it has also been suggested that the poet's relationship to the Symbolist heritage was a deeply problematic one. In this chapter we will consider the reverse side of this relationship: Hofmannsthal's ongoing critique of the artistic milieu of which both the Symbolists and he himself were a part. But this will require a widening of scope; while in dealing with the positive relationship we restricted our discussion to the major figures of Baudelaire, Verlaine, and Mallarmé, in discussing this critique we must include figures of lesser artistic rank, including some outside of France.

All of the major and minor French Symbolists can properly be viewed in the context of the broader European movement of Aestheticism. For present purposes, we will define this movement as consisting of all those writers in the latter part of the nineteenth century who subscribed to the doctrine of l'art pour l'art, who thus denied any social or political purpose to art and refused to have their art judged by any such non-aesthetic criteria. Of course, Kant and Schiller had insisted on functionlessness ("Nutzlosigkeit") as an essential characteristic of art; they too were concerned with defending the autonomy of art against incursions from non-aesthetic value systems. But this implied for them no denigration of the realms of social and political action, whereas for the Aestheticist writers of the later nineteenth century the worship of art was an attack, more or less explicit, on the materialism of their society.

In France, this attitude had its origins in the preface to Mademoiselle de Maupin by Théophile Gautier, the writer to whom Baudelaire dedicated Les Fleurs du Mal. Though in this as in every other question, one can cite contradictory passages in Baudelaire's writings, in this case some where he specifically rejects the doctrine of l'art pour l'art, most of his poetry and criticism is consistent with the doctrine, and certainly his influence on later generations lay in this direction. By the 1880s and 1890s, this orientation was taken for granted by all French anti-Naturalist writers, whether they called themselves Symbolistes, Décadents, or by any of a number of other names.

The situation in England is complicated somewhat by the fact that the father-figure of English Aestheticism, John Ruskin, was by no means unconcerned with social issues; his criticism came more and more to represent a critique of the pervasive ugliness resulting from the industrial and commercial spirit of England in the nineteenth century. Of course it is precisely the ascendancy of the materialist Utilitarian spirit, perceived as essentially hostile to poetry and the arts, which formed the background of all European Aestheticism. Where Ruskin differed from most of his successors (with the notable exception of William Morris) in all of Europe is that he applied his aesthetic concerns to the cause of social reform, in the hope of creating a new society in which the artist would once more have his place. By contrast, later figures such as the Pre-Raphaelites, the poet Swinburne, or the critic Pater, essentially turned their backs on current social reality and sought an alternative order in art, where they did not actually try, in conformance with Baudelaire's slogan "épatez le bourgeois," to affront middle-class sensibilities, as did the painter Whistler or the circle of Wilde and Beardsley in the 1890s.

The basic features of this movement are well known, especially through the life and work of Oscar Wilde in England or the figure of Des Esseintes from the novel <u>A Rebours</u> by Joris-Karl Huysmans in France. These artists were united in an aristocratic disdain for the "public," a word which was invariably a term of abuse in their mouths. Though the alienation of the artist from his society was already evident in many of the Romantics around the turn of the previous century, these earlier writers turned away from an indifferent society towards nature, which they glorified as the source of eternal verities. The Aestheticists, by contrast, stated their clear preference for art and artifice over nature. Wilde's reversal of an old dictum in observing that nature imitates art -- a sentiment echoed by the young Hofmannsthal in the quote which opens this work -- actually originated with Goethe, who meant by this, as did Wilde, that works of art teach us to "see" nature in a new and far more vivid way.[1] But once again there is a marked difference in attitude, since Goethe implied no denigration of nature, and recognized that the art which helps us see a new beauty in nature is in turn inspired by natural beauty. By contrast, Wilde in his fictional dialogue "On the Decay of Lying" has Vivian pointedly refuse his friend's invitation to go outside to enjoy a lovely afternoon. An even more significant difference, as L. A. Willoughby points out, is that when Goethe and Schiller proclaimed the ideal of aesthetic education, they specifically included the moral dimension as an essential part of the aesthetic, a dimension explicitly rejected by Wilde.

Following from this attitude is a preference for inorganic over organic forms, in particular a cult of precious stones and jewels, a preference for the exotic over the familiar, and a preference of archaic or historical settings and themes to anything contemporary. Following from this also is a cult of virginity: women are either admired as virginal aesthetic objects, or, to the extent that their sexuality comes into play, they are feared as destructive forces, as in Wilde's Salomé. But of course the consequence of eternal virginity is sterility, and this is a consequence which was to haunt artists well into the twentieth century. The most tragic and terrifying expression of this problem is in the figure of the composer Adrian Leverkühn in Thomas Mann's novel <u>Doktor Faustus</u>. Leverkühn has a naturally "virginal" disposition, that is an instinctive aversion to everything smacking of human warmth or sexuality accompanied by an affinity for all that is cold and non-human. And yet the threat of artistic sterility drives him into the arms of the prostitute from whom he knowingly contracts syphilis. The tragic inescapability of his dilemma is illustrated by the fact that the sexuality which releases his creative energy also propels him toward his own destruction.

* * *

In 1868, following the end of his stay in Tournon, which witnessed the greatest crisis of Mallarmé's poetic career, but also the conception and completion of the "Scène" from "Hérodiade" and the first version of "L'Après-midi d'un faune," the poet wrote to François Coppée on April 20 from Avignon:

> Pour moi, voici deux ans que j'ai commis le péché de voir le Rêve dans sa nudité idéale, tandis que je devais amonceler entre lui et moi un mystère de musique et d'oubli. Et maintenant, arrivé à la vision horrible d'une oeuvre pure, j'ai presque perdu la raison et le sens des paroles les plus familières.[2]

Anyone familiar with Hofmannsthal's "Ein Brief" will take

notice at these words. Indeed, one can only attribute to an obstinate unwillingness to see Hofmannsthal's real kinship to the French Symbolists the fact that this comparison has never (to my knowledge) been made previously. As with Hofmannsthal, a breakdown in cognition (j'ai presque perdu la raison) precedes or accompanies the crisis of language (et le sens des paroles les plus familières). Most importantly, in both cases the crisis of language stems from the perilous attempt to create a "poésie pure" using a language totally divorced from that of everyday communication, and in both cases the language has taken its revenge on the poet by withdrawing itself from him completely. Thus the Aestheticist poet who elevates sterility in the abstract is faced with the danger of sterility in his own work when he loses control of his artistic medium, language. I hasten to add that, especially in the case of "Ein Brief," I have done some extrapolating here. First of all, the sixteenth-century Lord Chandos is not engaged in writing a "poésie pure" in the modern sense; but the modern poet Hofmannsthal who conjured up this figure was doing just that, and there is little doubt that the experience of a loss of power over words, which he ascribes to Chandos, was one that the young poet himself had undergone. Still, and this is the second point, "Ein Brief" is of course not autobiography but fiction: Chandos' lapse into a state of total speechlessness (which is of course given the lie by his eloquence in describing this state) is in no way comparable to

Hofmannsthal's turn away from the lyric and toward the drama as his primary mode of expression. In this connection, it is appropriate to cite the words with which Richard Alewyn discusses the autobiographical element in the figure of Claudio from <u>Der Tor und der Tod</u>, words which apply equally to "Ein Brief":

> Gewiß erwartet man von einem Dichter seit einhundert oder zweihundert Jahren, daß er aus dem Vorrat seiner innern Möglichkeiten schöpft. . . . Aber Dichten heißt eben dieses: das nur Mögliche in den Stand der Wirklichkeit überführen. Darum ist eine dichterische Gestalt immer zugleich mehr und weniger als ihr Schöpfer. Mehr, weil sie nun wirklich, ganz und immer ist, was der Dichter nur möglich, teils und gelegentlich ist -- weniger, weil sie nur einer der Schatten ist, die ohne Zahl und Namen in seiner Seele hausen.[3]

Thus we must view Chandos and his situation as only one possibility within Hofmannsthal, a demon, if one will, that the poet exorcised in the composition of "Ein Brief," much as the young Goethe exorcised his private demon in writing <u>Die Leiden des jungen Werthers</u>.

For Hofmannsthal, as we shall see in the pages that follow, the danger of artistic sterility, following from the artist's rejection of colloquial speech in favor of a vision of "pure language," went hand in hand with the Aestheticist disdain for the larger community, and the cult of the sterile and inorganic. Together, these elements represented for him the negative side of the Symbolist heritage. In examining first several of the lyrical dramas and then a number of the essays ranging from the beginning to the end of his career, we will see how his critique of Aestheticism is accompanied by a continued insistence on the artistic worth of those products of this movement which reflect a real commitment on the part of a serious artist, as opposed to the work of poseurs and dilettantes.

Section One: Aesthetes and Artists in the Lyrical Dramas

In this section we will deal with those of Hofmannsthal's creative works in which the critique of Aestheticism is most explicit, the first three of the lyrical dramas: Gestern, Der Tod des Tizian, and Der Tor und Tod. In doing so, it will be necessary to cover ground which has been thoroughly treated by Richard Alewyn and Peter Szondi, in their excellent studies of the lyrical dramas. While trying to avoid mere repetition, I will emphasize those elements most directly relevant to our concerns, in particular the clear distinction made in all three plays between the aesthete and the genuine artist.

In Gestern, the aesthete Andrea clearly considers himself a patron of the arts. The stage direction describing Andrea's house which opens the play speaks of "reiche Architektur der sinkenden Renaissance, die Wände mit Stukkaturen und Grotesken geziert . . . eine Majolikaherme des Arentino"[4] etc. He counts a poet and a painter among his circle of friends. In true Wildean fashion he says: "Heut ist ein Tag Corregios, reif erglühend, / In ganzen Farben, lachend, prangend, blühend. . . ."[5] And yet the appearance is deceptive. When his friend, the painter Fortunio, asks what has become of a painting of his which had hung on Andrea's wall, and guesses correctly: "Es flog wohl fort . . . vor deiner Laune Wehen,"[6] Andrea answers, in some irritation:

> Hat nicht die Laune Wechsel, nicht die Kraft?
> Erwacht und stirbt nicht jede Leidenschaft? . . .
> Was macht das Alte gut und schlecht das Neue?
> Wer darf verlangen, wer versprechen Treue? . . .
> Ich will der freien Triebe freies Spiel,
> Beengt von keinem, auch nicht -- deinem Stil![7]

Somewhat later, the poet Fantasio expresses shock at his discovery that Andrea has just dismissed the architect who was in the middle of a construction project for him. In an even more revealing passage, Andrea explains why he has done this:

> . . . weil alles, was da wird und ragt,
> In Marmorformen reift -- mir nichts mehr sagt!
> Weil meine Schöpferkraft am Schaffen stirbt,
> Und die Erfüllung stets den Wunsch verdirbt.[8]

He goes on to express satisfaction at the prospect of the unfinished structure being reflected as a ruin in his pond; he calls it "totgeboren." To begin with, one can only smile at the presumption of Andrea in considering the labors of another artist to express his own "Schöpferkraft," since by his own admission he does not possess this power. But what he expresses here and in the earlier passage is nothing other than an impatience with the finished work of art itself, indeed with anything which does not mirror his mood of a particular moment. Thus Szondi's reference to "eine grundlegende Paradoxie des Ästhetismus, nämlich seine Kunstfeindlichkeit,"[9] as astonishing as it may appear at first glance, is fully borne out by the text. At least Andrea's brand of aestheticism conceals a genuine hositility to the finished work of art under the guise of a patron of the arts. Szondi points out how in this scene Andrea's "Absage an das Gestern" becomes a rejection of art as well, since it is in the nature of art to give concrete and enduring form to the inspiration of the moment. It is no accident that architecture is the example here, for it is architecture that most literally embodies the "concrete" nature of the finished work of art and thus which is most inimical to the impressionism of Andrea. Thus Andrea's aestheticism, which claims to create a work of art out of every moment of lived experience, in reality is destructive of both life and art. The facile distinction between life and art so current around the turn of the century is here implicitly rejected by Hofmannsthal; in denying life, one also denies art. By the same token, the creative artist, no matter how "aesthetic" his orientation, escapes the stigma of aestheticism insofar as he creates a work of art, his "deed" which is of equal validity to any action taken in life.

Before turning to <u>Der Tod des Tizian</u>, let us focus on two words that appear in these passages from <u>Gestern</u>. The first is "totgeboren," which Andrea applies to the "ruins" of his incomplete construction project. This would-be exponent of Lebensphilosophie is here too revealed as essentially life-denying in his obviously approving use of this term; the exponent of constant change and newness is shown to be threatened by the creation of something new. But the word "totgeboren" also ties in with the imagery of fertility and sterility which dominate such later works as Elektra and Die Frau ohne Schatten, which we will examine in the final chapter.

The other word is Treue. This is a concept of central importance in both Gestern and Der Tor und der Tod, and in both it is used primarily in its normal application to human relations. But in the passage quoted above, it is applied to the sphere of art. Defending his taking down of his friend's picture, Andrea demands: "Wer darf verlangen, wer versprechen Treue?" Not only is Andrea incapable of fidelity to a task he himself has originated -- the building project -- he cannot even remain faithful to a work of art created for him by a friend. But the creative artist needs this kind of "Treue" in the form of devotion to his work, and here again the aesthete is shown to be fundamentally distinct from the creative artist.

Let us turn now to Der Tod des Tizian. If Andrea's incapacity to deal with art was only a symptom of a larger problem, the inadequacy of his impressionist philosophy in dealing with life, in Der Tod des Tizian the opposition of the aesthete versus the artist is central to the play. The difference between the two plays is that whereas in Gestern the artists Fortunio and Fantasio are only foils for the aesthete Andrea, here it is the aesthetes who are Tizian's disciples who serve as foils for the artist; it is the figure of the dying Tizian who dominates the play, although he never appears on stage.

The disciples are aesthetes in a more conventional sense than is Andrea; we have no reason to doubt their devotion to the art of their master, but it is very clear that they are incapable of creating anything on their own. Tizian's death threatens them with "das tote, taube, dürre Weitersein." They have lived only through him and his work, and have sheltered themselves, out of fear disguised as contempt, from life in the city below. For them, who have not experienced life, death holds nothing but terror; but for Tizian, for whom life and art are inseparable, death holds no threat: "Indes er so dem Leben Leben gab, / Sprach er mit Ruhe viel von seinem Grab."[11] In all the speeches of Tizian's son and disciples in praise of the artist, the word <u>Leben</u> appears again and again ("Der Tizian sterben, der das Leben schafft," "Er hat den regungslosen Wald be<u>lebt</u>," etc.). At the end of his life the artist has a vision of the god Pan "der das Geheimnis ist von allem Leben," by contrast with which all his earlier life and work seems to pale. And yet even this earlier work is far more "alive" than anything his disciples can produce. This point is brought across most effectively in the exchange in which the youngest of the disciples, the sixteen-year-old

Gianino, relates the vision which he has had during the previous night. It is a vision of life which encompasses both nature and the lives of men in the city below. The other disciples, while admiring and envying in him visionary powers which they no longer possess ("Beneidenswert, der das noch erlebt"), react strongly against his inclusion of the city in his vision. Antonio says:

> Siehst du die Stadt, wie jetzt sie drunten ruht?
> Gehüllt in Duft und goldne Abendglut . . .
> In Schönheit lockend, feuchtverklärter Reinheit?
> Allein in diesem Duft, dem ahnungsvollen,
> Da wohnt die Häßlichkeit und die Gemeinheit,
> Und bei den Tieren wohnen dort die Tollen;
> Und was die Ferne weise dir verhüllt,
> Ist ekelhaft und trüb und schal erfüllt
> Von Wesen, die die Schönheit nicht erkennen
> Und ihre Welt mit unsren Worten nennen. . . .
> Denn unsre Wonne oder unsre Pein
> Hat mit der ihren nur das Wort gemein. . . .[12]

This is a classic statement of an aestheticism of the sort that Hofmannsthal found among his contemporaries in Vienna and in so much of the literature of his time. The attempt to view the city from a distance, in a haze which blurs all detail, is characteristic of this attitude. Antonio affects the voice of experience, but it is clear that he knows little of the real lives of men. Even the sixteen-year-old Gianino is aware of the discordant elements in this other world ("es wacht der Rausch, die Qual, / Der Haß, der Geist, das Blut") but he accepts them as part of life, which he understands by anticipation far better than the older disciples with their limited experience. Antonio reproaches the people below for their failure to recognize beauty, but it is questionable whether the disciples are really superior in that regard. As they remind us repeatedly, it is Tizian who has taught them to see beauty, but it is clear that they can only see it where he has revealed it to them. This point is made apparent when Paris ends his final speech with the words "Und wo wir Schönheit sehen, wird er sein," to which Desiderio says in reply:

> Er aber hat die Schönheit stets gesehen,
> Und jeder Augenblick war ihm Erfüllung,
> Indessen wir zu schaffen nicht verstehen
> Und hilflos harren müssen der Enthüllung. . . .[13]

One final comment on Antonio's speech: we see here the aesthete's scorn for colloquial speech (". . . ihre Welt mit unsren Worten nennen"). This turn of phrase is almost comical, for it is the disciples who describe their own world in words of common discourse. To summarize, in Der Tod des Tizian we see once more an opposition between the genuine artist, who is open to all forms of experience and transforms them all in his art, to whom nature, life, and art are inseparable, and the aesthete, who in his fearful separation of life from art is incapable of either.

In Der Tor und der Tod, it is the aesthete once more who appears on center stage; in fact, here there is no contrasting artist figure, and thus the opposition aesthete-artist is not nearly so explicit here as in the two earlier plays. But Der

<u>Tor und der Tod</u> does present the fullest exposition and critique of aestheticism as a philosophy or mode of life, and thus we must consider it briefly.

Though this play has a less remote historical setting and far less elaborate props than <u>Gestern</u>, Claudio too, like Andrea, has filled his living space with objects of art, which he addresses in the following passage:

> Ihr wart doch all einmal gefühlt,
> Gezeugt von zuckenden, lebendgen Launen,
> Vom großen Meer emporgespült,
> Und wie den Fisch das Netz, hat euch die Form gefangen![14]

He sees that this art is the product of life and feelings, but since he shares in neither, he sees their forms as prisons which trap the feelings as fish are caught in a net. To a painting of the Gioconda on the wall he says: "Gerad so viel verrietest du mir Leben, / Als fragend ich vermocht dir einzuweben!"[15] As Szondi points out, these lines might well serve as a judgment on Tizian's disciples who think they can find life in works of art without bringing any lived experience of their own to their interaction with the art. This is Claudio's predicament as well. Surveying the room around him, he says:

> Jetzt läßt der Lampe Glanz mich wieder sehen
> Die Rumpelkammer voller totem Tand,
> Wodurch ich doch mich einzuschleichen wähnte,
> Wenn ich den graden Weg auch nimmer fand
> In jenes Leben, das ich so ersehnte.[16]

Here as nowhere else in these plays the true motive for the aesthete's retreat is revealed: he takes refuge in art because he cannot find his way into life. Claudio is in general far more honest with himself, and has far more understanding of his own predicament, than do the aesthetes in the earlier plays. Where the disciples of Tizian tried to conceal their fear of the city below in a mask of contempt, Claudio, who also looks down at the city from a height, freely confesses his longing for the life of ordinary people. He knows that he has failed to live, and he knows why. In his words to Death, which could stand as a motto over all of Hofmannsthal's work, he points to what he has failed to do: "Ich will die Treue lernen, die der Halt / Von allem Leben ist."[17] To enter into life is to make commitments, to learn fidelity to the people one loves, to a principle, to one's work, and this is precisely what Claudio has never done; the ghostly visitors who follow the arrival of Death serve to confirm this fact.

Claudio's failure is the failure of all those who look to art as a substitute for what they have failed to find in life. He separates life from art, and this separation, as we have seen in Der Tod des Tizian, is fatal to both. The true artist faces life, accepts it with all its dark aspects, and elevates it into a work of art. Not only does this separation make Claudio incapable of creating art; by surrounding himself with works of art divorced from life, these lifeless forms become a trap which prevents him from growing into life. He is caught in the net of these forms, and thus he sees the original human content of the art caught in this same net, as in the metaphor quoted above.

* * *

We have seen how Hofmannsthal's first three lyric dramas embody a strong and explicit critique of aestheticism as a philosophy of life (as opposed to Aestheticism as a literary movement). Central to this critique is the concept of <u>Leben</u>: by his fear or inability to enter into life in the fullest sense, a sense which encompasses the ugly and the chaotic, the aesthete, who tries to create a realm of perfect beauty unspoiled by ugliness and vulgarity, succeeds only in creating a sterile environment, sterile in the literal sense of lifeless. Not only does he block himself off from an entry into life; but also the sterility of his life makes the works of art with which he surrounds himself lifeless as well. His failure to achieve <u>Treue</u> in his relations with others is a symptom of a more general problem: "die Unfähigkeit," as Hofmannsthal writes in <u>Ad me ipsum</u>, "jeden einzelnen Augenblick durch den Überschwang ins Reich des Ewigen zu heben."[18] One raises each individual moment into the realm of eternity through devotion to one's friends, but also in the creation of a work of art; in both cases it is the same quality of <u>Treue</u> that is required.

Section Two: Art, Life, and Language in the Essays

A. Essays of the "Lyrical Decade"

Though it is true, as mentioned in the introduction, that Hofmannsthal in his essays is curiously silent on the subject of the French Symbolists, the same cannot be said of the writers of Aestheticism as a whole. The first volume of his essays, including everything from the beginning of his career up to just before "Ein Brief," contains several essays devoted to figures associated with the English Aesthetic Movement, four essays on D'Annunzio, and several others which touch in one way or another on artists or problems associated with Aestheticism.

Before turning to the first of these essays, the one devoted to Swinburne, it may be useful to consider two passages in earlier essays, both written in 1891, and both of which we have mentioned earlier. The first is from the essay on Bahr's novel "Die Mutter," where, in a play on Goethe's famous aphorism, he speaks of dilettantism in connection with Romanticism:

> Denn Romantik . . . ist Krankheit der reinen Kunst, wie der Dilettantismus, das Anempfindungsvermögen, Krankheit des Empfindungsvermögens ist. Und die beiden, Romantik und Dilettantismus, sind immer zusammengegangen. . . . Man kann sich kein Milieu erschaffen, wie man sich keine Heimat machen kann; man kann keine fremden, angefühlten Empfindungen künstlerisch gestalten. Der Dilettantismus will beides.[19]

What is interesting here is that the dilettante is distinguished from the artist through his lack of authentic, lived experience; he must invent, or, more to the point, borrow the experience from others, hence the linguistic distinction between Empfindung and A̲nempfindung. The lack of artistic ability is thus intimately connected with a lack of experience, with remoteness from life. This is fully borne out by our discussion of Der Tod des Tizian in the preceding section.

Another suggestion of the same connection, though less explicit, occurs in the essay on Henri-Frédéric Amiel, "Das Tagebuch eines Willenskranken." Hofmannsthal calls him "dilettantenhaft" and goes on to say:

> Die Wonnen des Künstler-Schöpfers? . . . Ihrer war nie ein Mensch weniger würdig. Gleichviel; alles, was die Natur einem empfänglichen, nachschaffenden Geist gewähren kann, durchströmte ihn, wenn er vor Tagesanbruch aufstand, um vor seinem Pult in stiller Ruhe Weltenreisen und Jahrtausende zu durchfliegen, in immer höheren und reineren Kreisen zu schweben. . . . Aber getrieben von dem Durste nach Unendlichkeit, von einem unstillbaren Bedürfnis nach dem Absoluten, nach der Totalität, hatte er den Boden verloren.[20]

This thirst for infinity and totality is accompanied by a remoteness from real life, as Hofmannsthal points out, and this condemns Amiel to an essentially imitative (nachschaffend) kind of creation. At another point Hofmannsthal says in a passage previously quoted, "Amiel hat zum großen Künstler nur eines gefehlt . . .: Können."[21] Thus we see that from the very beginning of his writing career, Hofmannsthal associated real artistic creativity with an engagement in life, and implied that anyone lacking the former would most likely be lacking in the latter as well.

The first essay we shall consider now is the one devoted to Swinburne, written in 1893. It is interesting to note that the British poet is mentioned, along with Baudelaire, Verlaine, Mallarmé, and Poe, in the diary entry of December 21, 1891, in which Hofmannsthal refers to his first meeting with Stefan George.[22] In the entry in <u>Ad me ipsum</u> which lists "Frühe Einflüsse,"[23] the same list appears, but with the single omission of Swinburne's name. And yet, Swinburne is the only one of these poets to whom Hofmannsthal devoted an entire essay. We referred in the introduction to the curious fact that this prolific essayist should have maintained an almost total silence concerning those poets whom he later admitted had been his most important early influences;[24] in the light of this, we are led to suspect that Hofmannsthal wrote essays only on those contemporary writers with whom he could somehow "come to terms," and whose work thus did not provide any really fruitful challenge to his own. Whatever admiration he felt for the work of such artists, they clearly represented a path he was determined not to follow, and the essay was the ideal form in which to express both his admiration and his critique. In the case of Baudelaire, Verlaine, and Mallarmé, the impact of these men's work could not so simply be dealt with, and it is to Hofmannsthal's own creative work that we must look for his resolution of the challenge they posed to him, as we shall see in the final chapter.

But let us return to the essay at hand. Hofmannsthal begins with these words:

> Das moralische England besitzt eine Gruppe von Künstlern, denen der Geschmack für Moral und gesunden Gemeinsinn so sehr abgeht, daß sie für Saft und Sinn aller Poesie eine persönliche, tiefe und erregende Konzeption der Schönheit halten, der Schönheit an sich, der moralfremden, zweckfremden, lebenfremden.[25]

This is of course the English Aesthetic Movement, and its doctrine of l'art pour l'art, described in much the same terms used at the beginning of this chapter. The term "lebenfremd" reminds us of the aesthetes in the lyrical dramas, and as we might expect, the word Leben appears frequently:

> Diese Künstler . . . gehen nicht von der Natur zur Kunst, sondern umgekehrt. . . . Ihnen wird das Leben erst lebendig, wenn es durch irgendeine Kunst hindurchgegangen ist, Stil und Gesinnung empfangen hat.[26]

Here the word is used as practically synonymous with nature, with all that is not art or artifice, and the statement he makes describes the position of Wilde referred to earlier, as well as Hofmannsthal's own attitude in the earlier essay "Südfranzösische Eindrücke." Later in the Swinburne essay the word Leben appears in a somewhat different sense, when he speaks of the "künstlich verdunkelten Zimmer" in which the artist encloses himself:

> In Wirklichkeit aber rollt draußen das rasselnde, gellende, brutale und formlose Leben. An den Scheiben trommelt ein harter Wind, der mit Staub, Rauch und unharmonischem Lärm erfüllt ist, dem aufregenden Geschrei vieler Menschen, die am Leben leiden.
> Es herrscht ein gegenseitiges Mißtrauen und ein gewisser Mangel an Verständnis zwischen den Menschen in dem Zimmer und den Menschen auf der Straße.
> Diese Künstler kommen . . . nicht vom Leben her: was sie schaffen, dringt nicht ins Leben. "Was sie schaffen," sagen die auf der Straße, "sind lächerliche und verwerfliche Gefäße der Üppigkeit und der Eitelkeit."[27]

Here <u>Leben</u> refers to the world of man, with its brutality, loudness, and resistance to aesthetic form, the life in the city feared by the disciples of Tizian. What is significant here is that despite Hofmannsthal's high opinion of the art of Swinburne and other artists in the group he speaks of -- which becomes apparent in the second part of this essay and in later essays -- he focuses on the mutual incomprehension existing between these artists and ordinary men, not as proof of the inescapable vulgarity of ordinary men, as Wilde would have done, but as an implicit censure of these artists. This point must be emphasized, for even some sympathetic critics, who recognize Hofmannsthal's turn away from Aestheticism in his later years, nevertheless persist in regarding the young poet of the early 1890s as essentially in sympathy with the Aestheticism and "Décadence" of his contemporaries. This is no doubt due largely to the fact that the lines of battle between aesthetes and "Philistines" were rather sharply drawn at this time, and someone who, as did Hofmannsthal, expressed some sympathy for the former was (and often still is) assumed to defend all of their attitudes. But this incomprehension is also due in part to Hofmannsthal's own ambivalence. He seems to defend Swinburne against the man on the street, accepting the mocking reference to his works as vessels (Gefäße) when he goes on to say:

> Da ist unter ihnen einer, der füllt diese zierlichen und zerbrechlichen Gefäße mit so dunkelglühendem, so starkem Wein des Lebens, gepreßt aus den Trauben, aus denen rätselhaft gemischt dionysische Lust und Qual und Tanz und Wahnsinn quillt, füllt sie mit so aufwühlenden Lauten der Seele und solcher Beredsamkeit der Sinne, daß man ihn nicht länger übersehen kann.[28]

Here we find <u>Leben</u> used in still another sense; it is the vitalistic, Dionysian conception of life common to the <u>Lebensphilosophie</u> which was fashionable at the time, and which was derived largely from Nietzsche. The metaphor of Swinburne's poems as precious and fragile vessels containing the wine of life intensely experienced is appropriate for much of the best art of the Aesthetic Movement, and the idea of life here is very similar to that exemplified in the figure of the "Erbe" in the poem "Lebenslied," as well as the madman in <u>Das kleine Welttheater</u>.

It is worth stopping here for a moment to consider the variety of meanings attached to the word "Leben" that we have encountered so far. Understandably, much has been written about this word in the work of the young poet, but much of this has served only to obscure the issue by setting up an excessively schematic progression of mutually exclusive concepts which is claimed to take place in the course of Hofmannsthal's work during the 1890s.[29] It seems to me far more accurate and useful to view Hofmannsthal's use of the word as composed, from the beginning, of three essential elements, all of which we have encountered in the Swinburne essay: first, life in the most literal sense of the word, as nature, as all that is organic, as opposed to the sterile or inorganic; second, life in its essentially social sense, as ethical commitment to one's fellow men, as opposed to the enforced isolation of the aesthete; and finally, life in the essentially vitalistic sense of Lebensphilosophie, as opposed to all that is timid or life-denying. As one follows the course of Hofmannsthal's work, one certainly detects a deemphasis of the last meaning in favor of the second, but in this early stage it is necessary, as we have seen, to be aware of all three meanings.

If Hofmannsthal's ambivalence is reflected in the fact that he acknowledges Swinburne to be "lebenfremd" in the first two senses but not in the third, the ambivalence is not resolved through this distinction. Where earlier Hofmannsthal had implied that Swinburne's poetry was filled with the wine of Dionysian life, later he suggests that its content is far more

Apollonian:

> Es ist der raffinierte, unvergleichliche Reiz
> [seiner] Technik, daß sie uns unaufhörlich die
> Erinnerung an Kunstwerke weckt und daß ihr
> rohes Material schon stilisierte, kunstver-
> klärte Schönheit ist. . . .[30]

"Stilisierte, kunstverklärte Schönheit" is the material and the goal of Swinburne's verse. This is applied especially to the treatment of the beloved lady in the poetry, and also in the painting of Burne-Jones and the Pre-Raphaelites. Hofmannsthal continues:

> Der Inhalt dieser schönen Formen ist eine heiße
> und tiefe Erotik, ein Dienst der Liebe, so
> tieftastend, mit solchem Reichtum der Töne, so
> mystischer Eindringlichkeit, daß er im Bilde
> der Liebesrätsel die ganzen Rätsel des Lebens
> anzufassen scheint.
>   Was hier Liebe heißt, ist eine vielnamige
> Gottheit, und ihr Dienst kann wohl der Inhalt
> eines ganzen Lebens sein.
>   Es ist die allbelebende Venus, die "allnäh-
> rende, allbeseelende Mutter" des Lukrez, die
> vergötterte Leidenschaft, die Daseinserhöherin,
> die durch das Blut die Seele weckt.[31]

Here Hofmannsthal depicts the neo-medieval "Liebesdienst" of Swinburne and the Pre-Raphaelites in surprisingly uncritical, even rhapsodic language; nevertheless, one is struck by the contrast between this and the immediately preceding reference to the "opalinen Augen" of one of Burne-Jones' female portraits, or the statement at the beginning of the essay, "Beim Anblick irgendeines jungen Mädchens werden [diese Künstler] an die schlanken priesterlichen Gestalten einer griechischen

Amphore denken."³² In spite of the talk of a "heiße und tiefe Erotik," one suspects that what these artists worshipped was an ideal of pure beauty, rather than a flesh and blood woman; despite the reference to Lucretius' "allnährende, allbeseelende Mutter," with its suggestion of organicity and fertility, they are all too ready to compare a woman to an amphora, to speak of her eyes as precious stones. What I am doing here, I should like to emphasize, is not correcting Hofmannsthal's view of these artists through an examination of their works, but merely pointing out the contradiction inherent in his comments. On the one hand, he greatly admired this art; on the other, it was his conviction that all genuine art is infused with life, and yet he knew and could sense that these artists were "lebenfremd." If this ambivalence leads to a certain conceptual confusion in the essay, it also makes it a very rich and vivid appreciation of Swinburne's art.

Though Hofmannsthal clearly is thinking, in part, of the Pre-Raphaelites when he discusses the English Aesthetic Movement in at least implicitly critical terms in the first part of the Swinburne essay, the 1894 essay dealing specifically with the Pre-Raphaelites, "Über moderne englische Malerei," is almost entirely laudatory. He points to Dante as the source of their inspiration, and quoting from Pater's famous evocation of the Gioconda, praises the "vollendete Durchseelung des Leiblichen"³³ in their painting, their ability to express beauty of the soul in bodily form. Speaking of the figures in

Pre-Raphaelite paintings, Hofmannsthal says:

> Diese Wesen haben sich untereinander nichts zu sagen; sie fügen einander kein Gutes und kein Schlimmes zu; daß sie sind, ist alles, was sie voneinander wissen. Die Region des Dramatischen liegt anderswo, der Oberfläche näher. . . .[34]

Though this is not a critical statement, it appears a somewhat ambivalent one in the light of what we have already seen of Hofmannsthal's development. These men and women exist in the state of self-enclosure which he was later to call Praeexistenz, a state whose problematic nature we have already noted. And as we have seen, it was precisely to the "Region des Dramatischen" that Hofmannsthal was to turn as a way of breaking into Existenz, into social commitment. And though he seems to suggest in this passage that the dramatic is more superficial (oberflächlich), in the pejorative sense of the word, in his Buch der Freunde can be found the aphorism: "Die Tiefe muß man verstecken. Wo? An der Oberfläche."[35]

There is no escaping, however, the overwhelmingly positive tone of this essay. While the most directly critical comment is the admission, "Das Ganze hat etwas Künstliches,"[36] Hofmannsthal more than makes up for this with some very high praise. Referring to the surprise of many people at Ruskin's turn to moral and social concerns in his later years, Hofmannsthal says:

> Der Übergang von intensiver Beschäftigung mit der Kunst zu irgendwelchem anderen hohen und priesterlichen Beruf sollte doch niemals wundernehmen. Zumal diese englische Kunst der psychisch-leiblichen Schönheit ist durch und durch ethisch. . . . Diese gemalten Menschen erziehen die Seele durch das Beispiel ihres edlen Betragens.[37]

Though elsewhere he admits the <u>Weltfremdheit</u> of these artists, and though he repeatedly insists that the realms of the ethical and social are inseparable, here he makes a case for the ethical nature of Pre-Raphaelite art. Although we see in this another example of the poet's ambivalence, it would not be fair to accuse him of total inconsistency. For if one examines the above passage carefully, it becomes apparent that it is precisely the "intensive Beschäftigung mit der Kunst," their creation of beautiful and noble figures, which constitutes the ethical element of their work. The aesthetes of the lyrical dramas never had this intense and active concern with art which, as is implied in the figure of Tizian, represents a path into life which is barred to the mere aesthete.

More than anywhere else, it is in the first three of the essays on the Italian poet and novelist Gabriele D'Annunzio, written in 1893, 1894, and 1896 respectively, that Hofmannthal's ambivalence concerning the art of Aestheticism is reflected and finally resolved. The first of these opens, as does the Swinburne essay, with an extended introduction in which the poet himself is not mentioned. Where the earlier essay had begun with a description of a foreign artistic movement, this begins with a description of Hofmannsthal's own generation, and in his use of the first person plural he seems to identify, at least to some degree, with what he describes:

> Wir haben aus den Toten unsere Abgötter gemacht . . . wir haben diese Schatten umgürtet mit höherer Schönheit und wundervollerer Kraft als das Leben erträgt: mit der Schönheit unserer Sehnsucht und der Kraft unserer Träume. Ja alle unsere Schönheits- und Glücksgedanken liefen fort von uns, fort aus dem Alltag, und halten Haus mit den schöneren Geschöpfen eines künstlichen Daseins. . . . Bei uns aber ist nichts zurückgeblieben als frierendes Leben, schale, öde Wirklichkeit, flügellahme Entsagung.³⁸

He clarifies this by pointing out that he is speaking not of the entire generation, but only of those few thousand, scattered through the cities of Europe, who represent the consciousness of the generation, the awareness of its uniqueness and modernity, which he describes as follows:

> Heute scheinen zwei Dinge modern zu sein: die Analyse des Lebens und die Flucht aus dem Leben. Gering ist die Freude an Handlung, am Zusammenspiel der äußeren und inneren Lebensmächte. . . . Man treibt Anatomie des eigenen Seelenlebens, oder man träumt.³⁹

These two tendencies Hofmannsthal sees reflected, respectively, in D'Annunzio's novellas and in his poetry. When one considers that these two drives are the decisive ones in Claudio, the protagonist of <u>Der Tor und der Tod</u>, it becomes apparent that Hofmannsthal has not placed D'Annunzio in an especially flattering context; nevertheless, there is still no explicit criticism here.

Later in the essay, Hofmannsthal compares D'Annunzio's "Roman Elegies" with their prototype, the "Römische Elegien" of Goethe. Though the outward situation of the two lovers is parallel to Goethe's, there is an enormous difference:

> Es ist [bei D'Annunzio] keine Liebe zu zweien, sondern ein schlafwandelnder, wundervoller Monolog. . . . Dem nervösen Romantiker ist die Liebe halb wundertätiges Madonnenbild, halb raffinierte Autosuggestion; unter den Händen Goethes war sie nichts als ein schöner Baum mit duftenden Blüten und saftigen Früchten, nach gesunden Bauernregeln gepflanzt, gepflegt und genossen.[40]

The "wundertätiges Madonnenbild" reminds us of similar descriptions in the Swinburne essay: in both cases a woman is worshipped as a demigod or admired as an object of beauty, but never met on a human level. In opposing to this Goethe's ideal, which is clearly meant as a corrective, an example of a healthier attitude, Hofmannsthal emphasizes to an unmistakable degree the <u>organic</u> aspect of Goethe's ideal of love in the image of the carefully tended tree. Far more than in the Swinburne essay, Hofmannsthal here expresses this fin-de-siècle worship of the beloved as ultimately a worship of the self, an inevitably sterile attitude. Here, as in the later essay, he expresses a great admiration for D'Annunzio's poetic talent, but even his description of the beauty of the Italian's creations has a cutting edge. Comparing them to the

"Schäferspiele" of the Renaissance, he says:

> Es gibt unzählige Dinge, die für uns nichts sind als Triumphzüge und Schäferspiele der Schönheit, inkarnierte Traumschönheit, von Sehnsucht und Ferne verklärt, Dinge, die wir herbeirufen, wenn unsere Gedanken nicht stark genug sind, die Schönheit des Lebens zu finden, und fortstreben, hinaus nach der künstlichen Schönheit der Träume.[41]

Although the essay closes with a sympathetic evocation of the beauty of this dream world, these words remain as a judgment pronounced in the name of life, not on an aesthete incapable of either life or art, but on a living artist whom Hofmannsthal greatly admired.

The second D'Annunzio essay, written two years later, differs from the first in its noticeably greater degree of detachment; where in the first he had identified himself with the generation whose attitudes and aspirations he saw exemplified in D'Annunzio, here he speaks as an objective critic, both in praise and in condemnation. In words strikingly reminiscent of the Swinburne essay, he says:

> [D'Annunzio's] Lebens- und Weltgefühl hat sich nicht am Leben und an der Welt entzündet, sondern an künstlichen Dingen: an dem größten Kunstwerk "Sprache," an den großen Bildern der früheren Epoche, und an anderen niederen Kunstwerken.[42]

He proceeds to elaborate on various writers and artists from whom D'Annunzio has learned, finally quoting a stanza of his poetry, on which he comments:

> Wie schön das ist! . . . Denn der es gemacht
> hat, den haben die Worte, mit denen wir die
> Lust und Schmerzen des Lebens nennen, erbeben
> gemacht, früher und stärker und tiefer als das
> Leben selber.⁴³

We are reminded here of the dual nature of language; the words which are generally used merely for "naming" something other, take on for the poet a life of their own. But here life has the last word, as Hofmannsthal goes on to say:

> Aber das Leben ist doch da. Es ist durch sein
> bloßes oppressives unentrinnbares Dasein unend-
> lich merkwürdiger als alles Künstliche und
> unendlich kräftiger, und zwingt. Es hat eine
> fürchterliche betäubende Fülle und eine fürch-
> terliche demoralisierende Öde. Mit diesen zwei
> Keulen schlägt es abwechselnd auf die Köpfe
> derer, die ihm nicht dienen. Die aber von
> Künstlichen zuerst herkommen, dienen ihm eben
> nicht.⁴⁴

This has the force of a definitive statement in favor of life, of worldly engagement as the only legitimate basis for a work of art: this is no more than he had already suggested in the lyrical dramas, but it was one thing thereby to criticize non-productive aesthetes, quite another to apply this in censure to an actual artist of recognized talent. Referring his previous comments specifically to D'Annunzio's own works, he says:

> Es ist sehr sonderbar, wenn einer in so starren
> Dingen das Bild seiner Vision der Welt findet,
> da doch im Dasein alles gleitet und fließt.
> Und es ist sehr charakteristisch, daß sich ihm
> in den steinernen, künstlichen Spuren einer
> vergangenen Zeit das Leben ankündigt. Es ist
> in der Tat etwas Starres und etwas Künstliches

in der Weltanschauung des Herrn D'Annunzio. . . .[45]

In this opposition between "starren Dingen," "steinernen, künstlichen Spuren" and existence where everything "gleitet und fließt," there is a suggestion once more of the contrast between inorganic and organic form; the lifelessness of the things favored by an artist seem symptomatic of his own estrangement from life. Though the essay ends once more with a tribute to the artist's gifts and hope for his future, the criticism here has incomparably greater sureness and severity than in the earlier essay.

If by the second of these essays Hofmannsthal had risen above his own ambivalence to see clearly the inherent limitations of the art of Aestheticism, it is in the third that he begins to suggest a way out of what he was later to call "Sackgasse des Ästhetismus." This third essay, written in 1896 for Die Zeit, the same Viennese journal in which the second essay had appeared, opens with essentially a restatement of the pronouncement made in the previous one:

> Die sämtlichen merkwürdigen Bücher des Herrn D'Annunzio hatten ihr Befremdliches, ja wenn man will ihr Entsetzliches und Grauenhaftes darin, daß sie von einem geschrieben waren, der nicht im Leben stand.[46]

Hofmannsthal apologizes to his readers for what he calls the "nur unsichere und wenig präzise Worte" with which he had articulated his misgivings in the previous essay, and announces that he has "in den mannigfaltigen Erfahrungen eines Jahres eine komplexe, wortlose Lehre empfangen, welche sich auf das Sittliche in jener Sache bezieht. . . ."[47] As early as 1893 he had noted in a diary entry his conviction that "Die Grundlage des Ästhetischen ist Sittlichkeit,"[48] but here for the first time he enunciates the same insight in his public voice. In a passage strikingly similar to the earlier one which we quoted from the Pre-Raphaelites essay, he says of the characters in D'Annunzio's novellas:

> Nie hatten sie in Wahrheit etwas miteinander zu tun: ihr einziges Erlebnis war immer, daß sie einander anschauten. An dem Anschauen ihrer trügerischen Schönheit berauschten sie sich und wurden groß, an dem Anschauen ihrer selbst vergingen sie schließlich.[49]

But where in the Pre-Raphaelites essay this was essentially a descriptive statement, here it is clearly said in censure of this narcissistic tendency.

But here the solution is given:

> Ins Leben kommt ein Mensch dadurch, daß er etwas tut. Und die Männer und Frauen in den Büchern von D'Annunzio tuen nichts.[50]

It is through the deed, through active involvement in life, that one escapes from the narcissistic and ultimately self-defeating morass of the isolated, "aesthetic" existence. The remainder of the essay is devoted to an analysis of the new novel, Le Virgini delle Rocce, seen as D'Annunzio's attempt to break through in precisely the way indicated by Hofmannsthal. Without following his whole account of the novel, it will be useful to focus on several passages. Speaking of the hero of the novel, Hofmannsthal says:

> Er stellt sich allein, weil er anfängt zu fühlen, daß der Kontakt der Menge <u>unfruchtbar</u> macht. In seinem dürren Hochmut könnte er leicht häßlich und widerwärtig sein, aber manchmal macht seine Seele in einem der langen <u>sterilen</u> Monologe eine plötzliche Bewegung. . . .[51] (emphasis added)

I have emphasized what I find to be the crucial words in this passage: the hero fears that contact with people will make him "unfruchtbar," but the reference to his "dürrem Hochmute" and "sterilen Monologen" make it plain that it is precisely his arrogant avoidance of people that has had this result. The imagery of fertility suggested by these adjectives becomes explicit later in Hofmannsthal's account of the novel:

> Um seine Kraft, die das Göttliche an ihm ist, recht zu erkennen, hat er sie in Gedanken aus seinem Wesen herausgelöst und nennt sie sein ungeborenes Kind. . . . Der junge Adelige, der ein Künstler ist, wünscht einen Sohn zu haben, der ihm ähnlich sei. Das ist die ewige Weise, wie das Leben in uns sich zu erneuern strebt. Im Leben eines Menschen aber stellt dieser Wunsch . . . das innigste Bedürfnis vor, sich mit dem Dasein zu verknüpfen: Seinem ungeborenen Sohn eine Mutter suchen, heißt die Tat suchen, in der man seine Kraft hergeben und lebendig werden kann.[52]

It is hard to say if the child is a metaphor for the deed, or vice versa, but the importance of both is the same: they are means of joining one's self with life and bringing one's own powers out of a purely potential state into fruition. This "organic" aspect of action is constantly emphasized:

> D'Annunzio hat ein und dasselbe Wort für die Sträucher, die ihre Frucht gebären, und für die Seelen, die ihre Kraft in einer Handlung an den Tag bringen: beides heißt esprimere. <u>So dürstet, wie der Held, die ganze Landschaft nach dem Tun</u>.[53]

And yet, to these two paths into life, one's deed and one's child, we must add a third: the artist's finished work, which is both his deed and his child. This is clearly implied in this essay, and is confirmed in <u>Ad me ipsum</u> where Hofmannsthal lists the three paths

> . . . zum Sozialen als Weg zum höheren Selbst:
> . . . a) durch die Tat   b) durch das Werk
>   c) durch das Kind[54]

It is in this way that the creative artist justifies himself in the face of life; the genuine work is his "deed" and his "child," and it constitutes his breakthrough from narcissistic self-enclosure into life.

This explains the judgments which Hofmannsthal expresses in the two essays of this period devoted to poets who can certainly be called Symbolists: Francis Vielé-Griffin and Stefan George. We have already referred to the 1895 essay on this American-born minor Symbolist poet. Hofmannsthal condemns him with unusual harshness as derivative from Verlaine, totally lacking in the authenticity of lived experience, and as an example of what Hofmannsthal calls "journalistisches Denken." Further on he says:

> Man wird in den Werken von Swinburne und denen, die ihm nachahmen, dieses Element bemerkt haben, nämlich daß Poesie und Malerei sich gegeneinander neigen, um aus dem Mitschwingen der Stileindrücke einen raffinierten Reiz zu ziehen. Nichts aber wirkt verletzender als solche Raffinements, wenn sie nicht mit dem Geschmack und der triumphierenden Überlegenheit des Meisters angewendet werden.[55]

If the poetic gifts of a Swinburne can justify the refinement and exclusivity of his poetry, these traits are exposed without pity in the work of second-rate artists.

The 1896 essay on George, "Gedichte von Stefan George," is laudatory to an even greater degree than the Pre-Raphaelites essay. Where in the latter he had mentioned several traits which in a later context clearly became grounds for censure, in this essay he seems to endorse George's life, works, and attitudes in toto. A sample:

> Nur, da das Publikum überhaupt nicht mehr gewöhnt ist, daß in irgendeinem Ton zu ihm geredet wird, und völlig verlernt hat, die Töne zu unterscheiden, so sei hier kurz gesagt, daß die in Rede stehende Gedichte einen eigenen Ton haben, was in der Poesie und mutatis mutandis in allen Künsten das einzige ist, worauf es ankommt und wodurch sich das Etwas vom Nichts, das Wesentliche vom Scheinhaften, das Lebensfähige vom Totgeborenen unterscheiden.[56]

It is precisely the tone of this passage which is surprising after all we have seen: not only does Hofmannsthal endorse the haughty disdain for the public characteristic of George and his circle, he seems to adopt it himself in the rather arrogant tone which dominates much of the essay. And yet, he does praise George in the same organic terms we have encountered in other essays: it is an authentic tone, or its absence, in an artist's work which makes it either <u>lebensfähig</u> or <u>totgeboren</u>.

Shortly thereafter appears a sentence which seems to contradict directly all that has been said in earlier essays: "Es ist ein Hauptmerkmal der schlechten Bücher unserer Zeit, daß sie gar keine Entfernung vom Leben haben. . . ."[57] But he then continues:

> Diese Gedichte speien freilich nicht das gierig verschluckte Leben in ganzen Brocken von Sensationen von sich . . ., aber sie sind ganz mit Leben durchdrungen, und es ist gar nicht völlig aus ihnen herauszuwickeln.[58]

Thus a certain amount of detachment from life is permitted, even necessary for the artist, so long as life is present in his work.

The last of the essays from the 1890s we will consider is "Poesie und Leben," a shortened version of a speech given in 1896 before a group of Hofmannsthal's contemporaries in Vienna. This essay continues, to a large degree, both the tone and the argument of the George essay. In the opening paragraph Hofmannsthal manages to imply that his audience understands nothing whatever about the art of poetry, that their thinking on the subject is so hopelessly befuddled with false concepts that he despairs of communicating any sense of his art to them. After he has thus reduced his audience to size, he presents them with this definition of a poem:

> Ich weiß nicht, ob Ihnen unter all dem ermüdenden Geschwätz von Individualität, Stil, Gesinnung, Stimmung und so fort nicht das Bewußtsein dafür abhanden gekommen ist, daß das Material der Poesie die Worte sind, daß ein Gedicht ein gewichtloses Gewebe aus Worten ist, die durch ihre Anordnung, ihren Klang und ihren Inhalt, indem sie die Erinnerung an Sichtbares und die Erinnerung an Hörbares mit dem Element der Bewegung verbinden, einen genau umschriebenen, traumhaft deutlichen, flüchtigen Seelenzustand hervorrufen, den wir Stimmung nennen.[59]

In no other passage from the essays of this decade is the influence of French Symbolism more clearly to be seen than here. This cool, detached view of the poem as an artful combination of words arranged to produce a desired effect would indeed seem strange to a group of people schooled only in German poetry, but it is a view quite characteristic of contemporary poets in France, thanks to the influence of Baudelaire and Mallarmé (who in turn both admitted the derivation of their theory from Poe, particularly his essay "The Philosophy of Composition"). The idea of the poem evoking a certain "genau umschriebenen, traumhaft deutlichen, flüchtigen Seelenzustand" is a startling anticipation of the notion of the "état poétique" which Valéry later was to develop in his essays on poetry. Hofmannsthal continues:

> Die Worte sind alles, die Worte, mit denen man Gesehenes und Gehörtes zu einem neuen Dasein hervorrufen und nach inspirierten Gesetzen als ein Bewegtes vorspiegeln kann. Es führt von der Poesie kein direkter Weg ins Leben, aus dem Leben keiner in die Poesie. Das Wort als Träger eines Lebensinhaltes und das traumhafte Bruderwort, welches in einem Gedicht stehen kann, streben auseinander und schweben fremd aneinander vorüber. . . .[60]

Here is the dual nature of language once more, and here he emphasizes even more strongly the separation of poetry from life, the fundamental distinction between the word in a poem and the word "als Träger eines Lebensinhaltes." He goes on to quote approvingly from an unnamed author who says that:

> . . . den Wert der Dichtung entscheidet nicht der Sinn (sonst wäre sie etwa Weisheit, Gelahrtheit), sondern die Form, das heißt durchaus nichts Äußerliches, sondern jenes tief Erregende in Maß und Klang, wodurch zu allen Zeiten die Ursprünglichen, die Meister sich von den Nachfahren, den Künstlern zweiter Ordnung unterschieden haben.[61]

Once again, the insistence on form rather than content as the exclusive determinant of a poem's quality conforms entirely to Symbolist ideas, and is directly contrary to prevalent German notions, then as now. The Symbolist attack on rhetoric in poetry is also echoed by Hofmannsthal: "Das Rhetorische, wobei das Leben als Materie auftritt, und jene Reflexionen in getragener Sprache haben auf den Namen Gedicht keinen Anspruch."[62]

Much of this one might have expected, in light of Hofmannsthal's adoption of Symbolist poetic practice which we examined in the first chapter. But the insistence that life cannot make up the material of poetry does seem to contradict the critique of Aestheticism we have traced in the previous essays. But Hofmannsthal anticipates this objection as he says to his audience:

> Sie wundern sich über mich. Sie sind enttäuscht und finden, daß ich Ihnen das Leben aus der Poesie vertreibe.
> Sie wundern sich, daß Ihnen ein Dichter die Regeln lobt und in Wortfolgen und Maßen das Ganze der Poesie sieht. Es gibt aber schon zu viele Dilettanten, welche die Intentionen loben. . . . Auch seien Sie unbesorgt: ich werde Ihnen das Leben wiedergeben. Ich weiß, was das Leben mit der Kunst zu schaffen hat. Ich liebe das Leben, vielmehr ich liebe nichts mehr als das Leben.[63]

What he objects to is the naive expectation that life be present in a crudely naturalistic way: "Sie müssen sich abgewöhnen, zu verlangen, daß man mit roter Tinte schreibt, um glauben zu machen, man schreibe mit Blut."[64] But poetry is still intimately tied in with life in two ways: first of all, it is life that makes up the _content_ (as opposed to the medium or form) of a work of art, and it is only in its impact on living men, its _Wirkung_, that art is justified:

> . . . ich halte Wirkung für die Seele der Kunst, für ihre Seele und ihren Leib, für ihren Kern und ihre Schale, fur ihr ganzes völliges Wesen. Wenn sie nicht wirkte, wüßte ich nicht, wozu sie da wäre. Wenn sie aber durch das

> Leben wirkte, durch das Stoffliche in ihr,
> wüßte ich wieder nicht, wozu sie da wäre.⁶⁵

Only once in the essay is there an implicit criticism of Symbolist theory:

> Das Element der Dichtkunst ist ein Geistiges, es sind die schwebenden, die unendlich vieldeutigen, die zwischen Gott und Geschöpf hängenden Worte. Eine schöngesinnte Dichterschule der halbvergangenen Zeit hat viel Starrheit und enges Verstehen verschuldet, indem sie zu reichlich war im Vergleichen der Gedichte mit geschnittenen Steinen, Büsten, Juwelen und Bauwerken.⁶⁶

Though this does not necessarily refer exclusively to the French Symbolists, they are almost certainly among the poets to whom Hofmannsthal refers here. It is precisely in their partiality for the inorganic, frozen, and non-living that Hofmannsthal draws the line between himself and all the art of Aestheticism, including the Symbolists.

* * *

Summarizing the essays of the "lyrical decade," several points should be emphasized once more. As do the lyrical dramas, these essays bespeak a condemnation of those dilettantes and would-be artists for whom the cult of art and artifice is an escape from life, who can approach life only through the medium of art. Even artists whose work Hofmannsthal admires are censured for their remoteness from life, a remoteness which naturally is reflected in their art. The concept of life here is a complex one, as we have noted; at first it is strongly colored by the vitalistic notions of contemporary Lebensphilosophie, but this strain recedes during the course of the decade in favor of the ethical concept of life as social commitment in one form or another. Throughout this period, however, life is also conceived in its organic aspect, and in this sense it is opposed to the cult of the sterile and inorganic that bedevilled so much of the art of Aestheticism, including Symbolist poetry and theory. Yet except for this latter critique, the Symbolist concept of poetry is fully endorsed in the last of the essays examined, "Poesie und Leben"; if remoteness from life is considered in general to be an unhealthy condition for art, when Hofmannsthal speaks of the art closest to him, poetry, he defends the primacy of form as an element which is essentially removed from any direct connection with life. The work of Stefan George, the figure who was for Hofmannsthal (as we have noted) the living example of the Symbolist poet, is praised and defended without reservation. For it is the poet's work, his poem, which is the deed through which he enters into life, and it is only through obedience to the nature of his medium, to the poetic word as a constructive element of verse, that the poet can achieve this work.

B. Chandos and Beyond: Essays of the Later Years

In the 1896 essay "Poesie und Leben," which it is fair to

regard as the most explicit enunciation of his poetics during the "lyrical decade," Hofmannsthal specifically endorses the fundamental separation of poetic language from language as a medium of ordinary communication. But as Hofmannsthal surely realized even at the time, such a separation was bound to be problematic, for the words in a poem are still derived from the language of everyday communication, and the poem for him is justified only insofar as it is read and affects those who read it. Thus poetic language exists in a very delicate balance between, on the one hand, excessive closeness to ordinary discourse, viewed by both Hofmannsthal and Mallarmé as fundamentally debased, and on the other, such a great removal from ordinary discourse that the poet's control over his language, indeed his very sanity, is threatened. It is this danger which is suggested in Mallarmé's letter to Coppé, quoted earlier in this chapter, and which is given definitive artistic expression in "Ein Brief," the fictional letter of Lord Chandos to his patron Francis Bacon.

As Chandos recalls his former state, in which he produced his literary works, we recognize in his description all the features of <u>Praeexistenz</u>:

> Mir erschien damals in einer Art von andauernder Trunkenheit das ganze Dasein als eine große Einheit: geistige und körperliche Welt schien mir keinen Gegensatz zu bilden, ebensowenig höfisches und tierisches Wesen, Kunst und Unkunst, Einsamkeit und Gesellschaft: in allem fühlte ich Natur . . . und in aller Natur fühlte ich mich selber. . . .[67]

In this vision all existence is combined in the unity of nature, but in his intoxication the poet absorbed this all into himself: "Das Ich als Universum." But this state cannot last, and Chandos announces its collapse in words of shocking terseness: "Es ist mir völlig die Fähigkeit abhanden gekommen, über irgend etwas zusammenhängend zu denken oder zu sprechen." He then elaborates:

> Zuerst wurde es mir allmählich unmöglich, ein höheres oder allgemeineres Thema zu besprechen und dabei jene Worte in den Mund zu nehmen, deren sich doch alle Menschen ohne Bedenken geläufig zu bedienen pflegen. Ich empfand ein unerklärliches Unbehagen, die Worte "Geist," "Seele," oder "Körper" nur auszusprechen . . . die abstrakten Worte, deren sich doch die Zunge naturgemäß bedienen muß, um irgendwelches Urteil an den Tag zu geben, zerfielen mir im Munde wie modrige Pilze.[68]

But soon even the language of everyday conversation fails him:

> Mein Geist zwang mich, alle Dinge, die in einem solchen Gespräch vorkamen, in einer unheimlichen Nähe zu sehen. . . . Es gelang mir nicht mehr, [die Menschen und ihre Handlungen] mit dem vereinfachenden Blick der Gewohnheit zu erfassen. Es zerfiel mir alles in Teile, die Teile wieder in Teile, und nichts mehr ließ sich mit einem Begriff umspannen. Die einzelnen Worte schwammen um mich; sie gerannen zu Augen, die mich anstarrten und in die ich wieder hineinstarren muß: Wirbel sind sie, in die hinabzusehen mich schwindelt, die sich unaufhaltsam drehen und durch die hindurch man ins Leere kommt.[69]

Mallarmé and other Symbolist poets had disdained the "vereinfachenden Blick der Gewohnheit," and had analyzed ordinary language into its basic elements in their effort to create a fundamentally new poetic language; and Mallarmé had faced, and accepted, this néant which he, like Chandos, found behind these words deprived of all referential significance. But while Mallarmé's poetic art was founded on the edge of this abyss, Chandos lapses into unbroken silence from which there is no escape. Nevertheless, his new existence, thoughtless and speechless as it may be, is not without its redeeming moments:

> . . . es ist ja etwas völlig Unbenanntes und auch wohl kaum Benennbares, das in solchen Augenblicken, irgendeine Erscheinung meiner alltäglichen Umgebung mit einer überschwellenden Flut höheren Lebens wie ein Gefäß erfüllend, mir sich ankündigt.[70]

Theodore Ziolkowski has compared these moments of illumination to the "Epiphanies" of James Joyce, described in the sketches of this name and in Stephen Hero.[71] The parallel is indeed striking. However, it must be emphasized that while for Joyce the "epiphany" was a means of overcoming both the inadequacy of ordinary language and the perceived deadness of the empirical world, for Chandos they are only a recompense for his collapse into total artistic sterility. Though these epiphanies give Chandos some access to Existenz in a rather mystical sense of the word, the failure of his language seals his separation from Leben in the non-mystical sense of social engagement.

So much has been written on this work, and so much of it

misleading, that particular care should be taken to avoid false conclusions. Indeed, it would be virtually impossible to reduce "Ein Brief" to a categorical statement of any kind. An example of the dangers inherent in the state of <u>Praeexistenz</u>, certainly; an illustration of the infinitely precarious nature of our grasp on language, obviously. But to confuse the work with Hofmannsthal's own life and thereby to read it as a rejection of lyric poetry, is totally false. Hofmannsthal himself did not cease entirely to write lyric poems; of those he wrote after this time, "Vor Tag" and "Verse zum Gedächtnis des Schauspielers Joseph Kainz" must rank among his greatest. It is true that the two years preceding the writing of "Ein Brief" were rather unproductive ones for the poet, and that the experiences of Chandos are undoubtedly transpositions of similar experiences undergone by him. Still, one cannot forget that this is a fictional work, and that the artist Hofmannsthal was entering a productive new creative phase even as he depicted Chandos' lapse into artistic sterility. If one applies Chandos' experience to the poetic endeavor of a Mallarmé, one must read it not as a condemnation but as a warning of the tremendous danger of such an enterprise. As we will see in the essays that follow "Ein Brief," Hofmannsthal's adherence to Symbolist poetics remained unchanged in all its essentials even after the "Chandos crisis."

Hofmannsthal's primary concern with the drama from this

time onward is widely interpreted as a rejection not only of lyric poetry but also of the artistic influences of his youth, including the Symbolists. A glance at the 1903 essay "Die Bühne als Traumbild," however, should suffice to demonstrate that rather than abandoning the poetics of Symbolism, he carried them into the new genre of drama. As we have seen, Symbolist drama, far from being a contradiction in terms, was a very real force on the European stage at this time, as exemplified above all in the work of Maurice Maeterlinck. It is no accident that the only dramatist mentioned by name in this essay is Maeterlinck, for the essay is a clear endorsement of the anti-Naturalist style of set design which is still known as Symbolist. The stage must never present a literal version of reality; rather, it must be "etwas Wundervolles," it must have the imaginative fantasy and the compression of dream images. Above all, every detail must be significant: "Ein Bild schaffen, auf dem nicht Fußbreit ohne Bedeutung ist, das ist alles."[72] Normal relations of size and proportion need not be followed:

> . . . wer heißt den, der eine Bühne aufbaut, zwischen selig wandelnden Menschen und den Blumen die Schranken von Groß und Klein aufrichten, welche die Wirklichkeit -- die Wirklichkeit? -- einhält.[73]

In the most explicit rejection of the Naturalist insistence on reality as the only criterion, he goes on to say:

> Denn die Welt ist nur Wirklichkeit, ihr Abglanz
> aber ist unendliche Möglichkeit, und dies ist
> die Beute, auf welche die Seele sich stürzt aus
> ihren tiefsten Höhlen hervor.[74]

One suspects that he would have modified these prescriptions somewhat in the case of his social comedies of later years, though they could be applied to any of his dramas from the adaptations of Greek drama written around this time up to the final version of <u>Der Turm</u> in 1927. The point is that the turn to drama by no means implied a turn away from the ideals of dream and suggestion favored by the Symbolists, nor did it imply an acceptance of the Naturalist insistence on literal reality.

In the "Gespräch über Gedichte," also composed in the year 1903, Hofmannsthal returns to lyric poetry as the subject of discussion, and once more his views coincide rather exactly with Symbolist teachings. It is written, as are several of the essays in the second volume of Hofmannsthal's prose works, in the form of a fictional dialogue, this one between two young men named Gabriel and Clemens. It soon becomes apparent that while Gabriel is the mouthpiece for the poet's own Symbolist views, Clemens (who perhaps intentionally bears the first name of the most "romantic" of German lyric poets) represents traditional German views on poetry, and his bewilderment at the views expressed by Gabriel, together with the opening quotation from Hebbel (to the effect that aside from the poets themselves, there are only a handful of men in Germany who understand the first thing about poetry), suggest once more the haughty arrogance of the poet vis-à-vis an uncomprehending public which we saw in the earlier essays "Poesie und Leben" and "Gedichte von Stefan George," and which is so characteristic of George and his circle, as reflected by their pronouncements in Blätter für die Kunst. Indeed, the dialogue begins as Gabriel reads Clemens several excerpts from George's newly published Das Jahr der Seele. Commenting on the title of the work, Gabriel says:

> Diese Jahreszeiten, diese Landschaften sind nichts als die Träger des Anderen.
> Sind nicht die Gefühle, die Halbgefühle, alle die geheimsten und tiefsten Zustände unseres Inneren in der seltsamsten Weise mit einer Landschaft verflochten, mit einer Beschaffenheit in der Luft, mit einem Hauch?[75]

This is of course the doctrine of correspondences between outer and inner reality enunciated in Baudelaire's famous sonnet and adopted by Mallarmé and later Symbolists as one of the central points in their aesthetic.

The core of the dialogue is a discussion of the symbol, following from Clemens' observation that poetry "setzt eine Sache für die andere," a notion that Gabriel denies:

> Niemals setzt die Poesie eine Sache für eine andere, denn es ist gerade die Poesie, welche fieberhaft bestrebt ist, die Sache selbst zu setzen, mit einer ganz anderen Energie als die stumpfe Alltagssprache, mit einer ganz anderen Zauberkraft als die schwächliche Terminologie der Wissenschaft.[76]

Referring to a poem by Hebbel about a pair of swans, Clemens, who by now has grown rather confused, asks: "Und diese Schwäne? Sie sind ein Symbol? Sie bedeuten--," at which point Gabriel interrupts him to say:

> Ja, sie bedeuten, aber sprich es nicht aus, was sie bedeuten: was immer du sagen wolltest, es wäre unrichtig. Sie bedeuten hier nichts als sich selber: Schwäne. Schwäne, aber freilich gesehen mit den Augen der Poesie, die jedes Ding mit allen Wundern seines Daseins umgibt. . . . Gesehen mit diesen Augen sind die Tiere die eigentlichen Hieroglyphen, sind sie lebendige geheimnisvolle Chiffern, mit denen Gott unaussprechliche Dinge in die Welt geschrieben hat.[77]

The idea of objects of nature as hieroglyphs or chiffres of an ineffable underlying reality is familiar from Novalis, but it is also present in the Symbolists. In his article on Victor Hugo, Baudelaire wrote that

> . . . tout, forme, mouvement, nombre, couleur, parfum, dans le spirituel comme dans le naturel, est significatif, réciproque, converse, correspondant. . . . tout est hiéroglyphe, et nous savons que les symboles ne sont obscurs que d'une manière relative, c'est-à-dire selon la pureté, la bonne volonté, ou la clairvoyance des âmes.[78]

This passage was of great importance to Mallarmé, leading him to the insight that poetry is not invented but discovered.[79]

To explain the nature of the symbol to his friend, Gabriel launches into an extended account of the first man to perform a blood sacrifice:

> Er vollbrachte eine symbolische Handlung. Er
> starb in dem Tiere, Clemens, weil er sich einen
> Augenblick lang in dies fremde Dasein aufgelöst
> hatte, weil einen Augeblick lang wirklich sein
> Blut aus der Kehle des Tieres gequollen war.[80]

The essence of the symbol, then, is a mystical identification with the object; a poetic symbol does not "stand for" something else, instead it invites the reader to fulfill this act of identification and thereby to experience the object "mit allen Wundern seines Daseins."

All this is completely in accord with Symbolist aesthetics. But there are a few hints in this essay of a divergence from certain aspects of Symbolism. Consider this passage:

> . . . es ist wundervoll, wie diese Verfassung
> unseres Daseins der Poesie entgegenkommt: denn
> nun darf sie, statt in der engen Kammer unseres
> Herzens, in der ganzen ungeheueren, unerschöpf-
> lichen Natur wohnen.[81]

Needless to say, it is hardly characteristic of Symbolism to place the locus of poetry in nature. Later on he says:

> Denn [die Poesie] hat keine Grenzen ihres
> Fluges, aber in ihrem Wesen ist sie begrenzt:
> wie könnte sie aus irgendeinem Abgrund der
> Welten etwas anderes zurückbringen als mensch-
> liche Gefühle, da sie doch selbst nichts
> anderes ist als die menschliche Sprache![82]

Here we see a striking change, not only from Symbolist theory, but also from his own earlier conceptions. We may regard this as the one really significant impact of the "Chandos crisis" on his poetic theory: the stress on the dual nature of language recedes in favor of the realization that poetry is based on the language of men, and dare not lose all contact with this colloquial speech. Obviously, this is an insight which was very helpful to the dramatist of later years.

One more passage is of interest. Clemens tries to defend the notion of a poem as a "geformter Gedanke," to which Gabriel replies:

> Ja, der Gedanke ist etwas Schönes und du hast so großes Recht, ihn der Perle und dem Edelstein zu vergleichen. Diesen beiden gleicht er, die schöner sind als alles Blühen und Leben, weil sie über das Blühen und Leben hinaus sind. Und für eine junge Welt, die daliegt in Blindheit, ist er das Wunder der Wunder. . . . Wir aber sind reicher an Gedanken, als der endlose Meeresstrand an Muscheln. Was uns not tut, ist der Hauch.[83]

Though the poems of the Symbolists were seldom "geformte Gedanken," the preference for precious stones over organic life is already familiar to us as a characteristic of the Symbolist aesthetic milieu. Here Hofmannsthal does not condemn these stones, or the thoughts they represent -- he even concedes they are more beautiful than "alles Blühen und Leben" -- but he asserts that at the present time what is needed is not <u>Gedanke</u> but <u>Hauch</u>, not inorganic but organic forms.

The image of precious stones, which was once used in an unmistakably positive sense to suggest the magical power of poetic language, appears in a less flattering context in "Sebastian Melmoth," the 1905 essay on the life of Oscar Wilde: "Die Edelsteine, in denen er vorgab mit Lust zu wühlen, waren wie gebrochene Augen, die erstarrt waren, weil sie den Anblick des Lebens nicht ertragen hatten."[84] Another step has been taken away from the Symbolist/Aestheticist glorification of the inorganic, which is here explicitly linked with the inability to face life. In general one can say of this essay that it speaks with far more critical detachment than any of the earlier essays on major figures of Aestheticism. And yet, there is also noticeable sympathy in his portrayal of Wilde as a tragic figure who sought out his own destruction as surely as did Oedipus, a sympathy which was hardly characteristic of most of his contemporaries.

In "Der Dichter und diese Zeit," a lecture held in 1906 or 1907, the mature Hofmannsthal speaks of the poet's position in the present age. The comparison with "Poesie und Leben," delivered on a similar occasion ten years earlier, is inevitable, and it reveals a marked change in attitude. If Hofmannsthal was to maintain to the end of his life a disdain for all that was dilettantish, inauthentic, or second-rate in art and among artists, the contemptuous attitude toward his audience, which was evident in the earlier essays, and even as late as the "Gespräch über Gedichte," is totally lacking in this lecture and, with few exceptions, in his work from this time on. The lecture is permeated with the realization that a poet depends on a receptive audience if his existence is to have any meaning. He even seeks to diminish the gap separating him from his audience by asserting, "Diese haarscharfe Absonderung des Dichters vom Nicht-Dichter erscheint mir gar nicht möglich."[85] A more appropriate distinction, he suggests, is that between a successful and an unsuccessful work of art, as he cites with approval Goethe's insight "daß ein unvollkommenes Kunstwerk nichts ist."[86]

But if a poet who reaches maturity in an Aestheticist milieu makes a break with this heritage in asserting the necessary ties which bind him to his audience, he is faced with the predicament which drove the poets of Aestheticism into their haughty isolation in the first place: the general public indifference to poetry. Hofmannsthal faces this dilemma and resolves it with this surprising assertion:

> . . . daß das Lesen, die maßlose Gewohnheit, die ungeheure Krankheit, wenn Sie wollen, des Lesens, dieses Phänomen unserer Zeit, das man zu sehr der Statistik und Handelskunde überläßt und dessen subtilere Seiten man zu wenig betrachtet, nichts anderes ausdrückt als eine unstillbare Sehnsucht nach dem Genießen von Poesie.[87]

In all the insatiable reading of newspapers, journals, novels, and a thousand other things which Hofmannsthal considers a characteristic phenomenon of the age, he sees an unconscious search for the binding and vivifying power that only poetry can give. Even the interest in pure science is an expression of the same impulse:

> Aber sind es denn nicht wirklich nur und allein die wenigen, welche in einer Wissenschaft arbeiten, die ihr wirkliches Wesen in ihr suchen, ihr strenges, abgeschlossenes, von einem Abgrund ewiger Kälte umflossenes Dasein -- und wäre für die unerprobten suchenden Seelen der vielen diese Kälte nicht so fürchterlich, daß sie sich daran verbrennen würden, und für ewig diesen Ort meiden?
> . . . es ist nicht die Sache der vielen, es kann nicht ihre Sache sein. Denn sie stehen im Leben, und aus der Wissenschaft, in ihrem reinen, strengen Sinn genommen, führt kein Weg ins Leben zurück. . . . Wonach ihre Sehnsucht geht, das sind die verknüpfenden Gefühle; die Weltgefühle, die Gedankengefühle sind es, gerade jene, welche auf ewig die wahre strenge Wissenschaft sich versagen muß, gerade jene, die allein der Dichter gibt.[88]

Of science it is said, as it was of art in the lecture ten years earlier, that there is no path leading from it into life. Here it is poetry that reaches into life because it is infused with life in a way pure science can never be.

The poet's role in the world is illustrated by a reference to the legend of St. Alexis, who returns to his own house in disguise and lives under the stairway as a silent observer, recognized by none. But he is more than just an observer; he is the focal point where all the conflicting currents of his time come together:

> Wie der innerste Sinn aller Menschen Zeit und Raum und die Welt der Dinge um sie her schafft, so schafft er aus Vergangenheit und Gegenwart, aus Tier und Mensch und Traum und Ding, aus Groß und Klein, aus Erhabenem und Nichtigem die Welt der Bezüge.[89]

This "world of relationships" has been compared to Baudelaire's "Correspondances,"[90] but Hofmannsthal's notion seems to me much less mystical and more worldly than Baudelaire's; rather than establishing correspondences between mental and external realities, the poet here binds together all things within the world. This idea, and the essay which contains it, constitutes what is perhaps Hofmannsthal's most moving expression of faith in poetry and art in the service of life, a position towards which he had been groping since his earliest essays.

In conclusion we will briefly examine a few of the essays in the final volume of Hofmannsthal's prose works, the one devoted to his work after World War I. In this final decade of his life, after the collapse of the political institution to the defense of which he had devoted so much of his energy, the poet's concern turns once more to the redeeming and constructive power of language. In one of the "Drei kleinen Betrachtungen" of 1921, entitled "Schöne Sprache," he quotes these words from a letter someone has written to him: "Die Sprache, an sich und zwecklos, soll und kann Gegenstand und Ausdruck einer Kunst sein. . . ." His reply is cautious:

> Gewiß, das ist ganz richtig, man darf das sagen, es deutet in die Richtung hin, wo die Wahrheit liegt, aber man müßte noch ein wenig in die Tiefe gehen, um auf die wirkliche Wahrheit zu kommen.[91]

He does not reject outright this essentially Symbolist view of language, but feels it needs elaboration and greater depth. Later he says:

> Auf Kontakt mit einem idealen Zuhörer läuft es bei ihnen allen hinaus. Dieser Zühorer ist so zu sprechen der Vertreter der Menschheit, und ihn mitzuschaffen und das Gefühl seiner Gegenwart lebendig zu erhalten, ist vielleicht das Feinste und Stärkste, was die schöpferische Kraft des Prosaikers zu leisten hat.[92]

While approving his correspondent's emphasis on form over content in language, Hofmannsthal once more insists on contact with at least an ideal reader as a necessary condition for "schöne Sprache."

In the "Ankündigung" for the Neue Deutsche Beiträge of 1922, Hofmannsthal refers to language as "der geistige Besitz der Nation" and says:

> . . . denn wo wäre, als in der Sprache, der geistige Besitz der Nation lebendig zu finden? Immerhin. Die Sprache, ja, sie ist Alles; aber darüber hinaus, dahinter ist noch etwas: die Wahrheit und das Geheimnis.[93]

As long as one's view of language is broad enough to include "die Wahrheit und das Geheimnis" which lies behind it, it is legitimate to say that language is everything. Here again he seems to be mediating between the Symbolist insistence on the primacy of language and his own conviction that language is essentially the property of the people and the nation bound together by that language.

Nowhere are these convictions more forcefully expressed

than in the 1927 essay, based on a lecture delivered to the students of the University of Munich, "Das Schrifttum als geistiger Raum der Nation." In it he speaks admiringly of the role that language and literature have played among the French:

> Die Literatur der Franzosen verbürgt ihnen ihre Wirklichkeit. Wo geglaubte Ganzheit des Daseins ist -- nicht Zerrissenheit -- , dort ist Wirklichkeit. Die Nation, durch ein unzerreißbares Gewebe des Sprachlich-Geistigen zusammengehalten, wird Glaubensgemeinschaft, in der das Ganze des natürlichen und kultürlichen Lebens einbeschlossen ist. . . .[94]

This binding power of a nation's linguistic and literary heritage, so characteristic of France, Hofmannsthal finds sadly lacking in the German cultural sphere:

> Wenden wir uns der eigenen Nation zu, so tönt uns freilich geradezu das Gegenteil jener Einhälligkeit entgegen. Von einer Zusammenfassung aller produktiven Geisteskräfte der Nation im Gebiete der Literatur kann keine Rede sein. . . . Jener Kreislauf zwischen dem Geistigen und dem Gesellschaftlichen, auf den dort alles hindrängt, in den schließlich alles einmündet, ihm wirkt hier der tiefste Instinkt entgegen.[95]

The critique that was earlier applied to the literature of Aestheticism -- its remoteness from social life -- is here applied to the German literary tradition. In view of this conjunction, it is not surprising to find, a few pages later, a hidden but unmistakable portrait of that most aesthetic and asocial of German poets, Stefan George. Of him it is said:

> Um die Sprache ringt er zuzeiten wirklich -- aber

> nicht mitzuwirken an der Schöpfung der Sprach-
> norm, in der die Nation zur wahren Einheit sich
> bindet, sondern als die magische Gewalt, die
> sie ist, will er sich sie dienstbar machen.
> . . . Zuzeiten wieder wird er die Herablassung
> des Sprechens verschmähen, wird er durch Krisen
> einer Sprachbezweiflung durchgehen, die ihre
> furchtbaren Spuren bis in die flackernden Züge
> seines Gesichtes zurücklassen wird, und wieder
> zuzeiten sich emporschwingen zu einer Ahnung
> der heilenden Funktion der Sprache, zur Er-
> schauung verwirklichbarer Maßgestalten.[96]

What began as a portrait of George could be said, by the end, of the young Hofmannsthal as well: in both cases it is a poet whose concern with language relates only to its magical powers, not to its role as the binding force of a nation. The same is of course true of the French Symbolists, who in this respect are not at all typical of their nation. Once more, this attitude is not criticized outright, but is combined as one element in the synthesis to produce the "konservative Revolution" which Hofmannsthal proclaims as his hope for the spiritual mission of Germany, a hope which was to be cruelly shattered by events only a few years later, events which Hofmannsthal mercifully did not live to witness.

Finally, we turn to an essay Hofmannsthal wrote in 1929, the last year of his life, "Einige Worte als Vorrede zu St.-J. Perse, 'Anabasis.'" It is only in this essay that Hofmannsthal breaks his long silence on the subject of the major French Symbolists.

> Wir sehen die französischen Dichter seit etwa
> vierzig Jahren in einem Kampf begriffen: wir

> müssen diesen Kampf und sein Ziel zu verstehen
> trachten. . . . Es geht um die französische
> Sprache in ihrer geheimsten Funktion, und
> dieser Kampf ist alt.[97]

He speaks of the characteristic rationality of the French, reflected in the victory of Malherbe over Régnier in the seventeenth century:

> . . . der verstandesmäßige Ton siegt über die
> emotionelle Schwingung. Das Gesetzmäßige wird
> für alle Zeit befestigt, das Unbewußte, das uns
> zu oft überflutet, wird hinabgedrückt. Die
> pragmatische Eindeutigkeit des Ausgesagten wird
> als Forderung statuiert, selbst der gleichnis-
> weise Ausdruck, die Metapher, sehr strengen
> Einschränkungen unterworfen.[98]

But this rigid attitude must inevitably provoke a reaction, in the nineteenth and twentieth as well as in the seventeenth century:

> Das geheime Leben der Sprache aber, von dem
> eine zarte innerste Vitalität der Nation ab-
> hängt, setzt sich zur Wehr. Jener alte Kampf,
> den im sechzehnten Jahrhundert die Pléïade ge-
> führt hatte -- Kampf um eine freie Syntax, um
> kühnere, vieldeutigere Metaphern, um eine Annä-
> herung an die Musik der eigenen Epoche --, wir
> sehen ihn zu Ende des neunzehnten Jahrhunderts
> sich erneuern. Mallarmé ist der große Führer
> und Doktrinär dieser Bewegung (aber seine Dok-
> trin gleicht seiner Poesie, sie vollzieht sich
> in Andeutung, und in ihr herrscht das Elimi-
> nieren der Präzision, des pragmatischen Zusam-
> menhangs, und nur um so größer und nachhaltiger
> ist ihre Wirkung). Aber vor Mallarmé gehen
> Baudelaire und Rimbaud, und der majestätische
> Fluß, die geheime Polyphonie des einen sowie
> das wilde Durchbrechen der Ordnungen bei dem
> andern, bei beiden ist es ein Sich-Annähern an
> den Bereich der Musik, das sie als Brüder zu
> Mallarmé stellt.[99]

The passionate struggle to preserve "das geheime Leben der Sprache," which Hofmannsthal sees the Symbolists as exemplifying, is here justified even in terms of service to the nation, whose "zarte innerste Vitalität" depends on this secret life of language. Hofmannsthal adds the names of Claudel and Valéry to those mentioned above, and summarizes:

> Ihnen allen geht es darum -- und welch eine Reihe der edelsten Namen haben wir aufgestellt -- , die lyrische Inspiration aus dem Innern der Sprache selbst zu erneuern.[100]

Here Hofmannsthal confirms the judgment which we formed through extrapolation from the essays of the lyrical decade: it is the intense seriousness of the major Symbolists' endeavor, their constant devotion to the craft of poetry, which raises them above the dilettantes and poseurs of their Aestheticist milieu into the ranks of truly great artists.

One can only speculate as to why Hofmannsthal never saw fit to discuss these writers until the end of his life. Perhaps it was not until this time that he felt a sufficient detachment from the period of his life in which their influence was the strongest, that he sensed a resolution finally of the lifelong struggle which the challenge of these writers provoked in his own work. Perhaps, considering his comments in the Vielé-Griffin essay and in diary entries from the nineties, he felt that the influence of these writers was inevitably destructive to all but the greatest talents, and thus hesitated to proclaim their art to a generation all too disposed to be influenced by it -- the new generation to whom he addressed his 1929 comments, he might have felt, was by contrast not attentive enough to the aesthetic concerns of these writers. But perhaps it is because Baudelaire and Mallarmé, these high priests of the sterile and inorganic, had paradoxically revealed the fertility of their own art in the enormous and beneficial impact which the passing of time showed them to have had on a talented new generation of poets.

*   *   *

Thus we have seen that the poet's immersion in the magical power of language, divorced from its normal communicative value, can be a highly dangerous enterprise, as shown in "Ein Brief." Hofmannsthal's writing subsequent to 1902 is tempered by the awareness of this danger, and strengthened by the attempt to view language as the force which binds a poet to his audience, rather than separating him from it. And yet this new emphasis goes hand in hand with a continued espousal of the aesthetics of Symbolism in all essential points, in the theatre as well as in poetry. The genuine poet, in his devotion to the craft of language, must inevitably serve the larger community, even if he appears to isolate himself from it. And thus we see an essential continuity from the earliest essays and lyrical dramas to the final essays: the claims of art and life, which in the work of so many of his contemporaries are hopelessly antithetical, are shown in Hofmannsthal's essays with increasing clarity to be fundamentally compatible.

NOTES

[1] See L. A. Willoughby, "Oscar Wilde and Goethe: The Life of Art and the Art of Life," Publications of the English Goethe Society, NS 35 (1965) 1-37.

[2] Stéphane Mallarmé, Correspondance 1862-1871, ed. Henri Mondor and Jean-Pierre Richard (Paris: Gallimard, 1959), p. 270.

[3] Richard Alewyn, Über Hugo von Hofmannsthal (Göttingen: Vandenhoeck & Ruprecht, 1958), p. 65.

[4] GLD, p. 139.

[5] GLD, p. 149.

[6] GLD, p. 155.

[7] GLD, p. 155.

[8] GLD, p. 160.

[9] Peter Szondi, Das lyrische Drama des Fin-de-siècle (Frankfurt: Suhrkamp, 1975), p. 186.

[10] Szondi, p. 187.

[11] GLD, p. 197.

[12] GLD, p. 190.

[13] GLD, p. 198.

[14] GLD, p. 203.

[15] GLD, p. 203.

[16] GLD, p. 202.

[17] GLD, p. 211.

[18] A, p. 215.

[19] PI, pp. 17-18.

[20] PI, p. 27.

[21] PI, pp. 29-30.

[22] A, p. 93.

[23] A, p. 237.

[24] T. S. Eliot, in the title essay of the volume To Criticize the Critic, points out that he never wrote anything about the French Symbolist poets who had the greatest influence on him. (New York: Farrar, Straus & Giroux, 1965), p. 22.

[25] PI, p. 99.

[26] PI, p. 99.

[27] PI, pp. 100-101.

[28] PI, p. 101.

[29] An example of this is an essay widely considered to be the classic treatment of the subject, "Die Idee des Lebens in Hofmannsthals Jugendwerk 1890-1900" by Andrew O. Jaszi (Germanic Review, 24, No. 2 [1961], 69-95), who assumes that Hofmannsthal until 1896 was entirely sympathetic to what Jaszi calls literary "Decadence," a view supported by a total misreading of Der Tod des Tizian as an endorsement of the views expressed by Tizian's disciples. See also Otto Friedrich Bollnow, "Der Lebensbegriff des jungen Hugo von Hofmannsthal," Unruhe und Geborgenheit im Weltbild neuerer Dichter (Stuttgart: Kohlhammer, 1953), pp. 15-30, and Steven P. Sondrup,

"The Contexts and Concepts of 'Leben' in the Poetry of Hugo von Hofmannsthal," Colloquia Germanica, 11 (1978), 289-297.

[30] PI, p. 103.

[31] PI, p. 104.

[32] PI, p. 99.

[33] PI, p. 199.

[34] PI, p. 195.

[35] A, p. 47.

[36] PI, p. 196.

[37] PI, p. 200.

[38] PI, pp. 147-48.

[39] PI, p. 149.

[40] PI, pp. 154-55.

[41] PI, p. 157.

[42] PI, p. 207.

[43] PI, p. 209.

[44] PI, p. 209.

[45] PI, pp. 210-11.

[46] PI, p. 233.

[47] PI, p. 233.

[48] A, p. 101.

[49] PI, p. 234.

[50] PI, p. 235.

[51] PI, p. 237.

[52] PI, pp. 237-38.

[53] PI, p. 239.

[54] A, p. 217.

[55] PI, p. 222.

[56] PI, p. 242.

[57] PI, p. 243.

[58] PI, p. 243.

[59] PI, p. 263.

[60] PI, p. 263.

[61] PI, p. 264.

[62] PI, p. 264.

[63] PI, p. 266.

[64] PI, p. 266.

[65] PI, p. 266.

[66] PI, pp. 266-67.

[67] PII, p. 10.

[68] PII, pp. 11-12.

[69] PII, p. 13.

[70] PII, p. 14.

[71] "James Joyces Epiphanie und die Überwindung der Wirklichkeit in der modernen deutschen Prosa," Deutsche Vierteljahrsschrift, 35, No. 4 (1961), 594-616.

[72] PII, p. 63.

[73] PII, p. 64.

[74] PII, p. 66.

[75] PII, p. 82.

[76] PII, p. 84.

[77] PII, pp. 86-87.

[78] Stéphane Mallarmé, Oeuvres Complètes, ed. Henri Mondor and G. Jean-Aubry (Paris: Gallimard, 1970), p. 705.

[79] Guy Michaud, Mallarmé, trans. Marie Collins and Bertha Humez (New York: New York University Press, 1965), p. 66.

[80] PII, p. 89.

[81] PII, p. 83.

[82] PII, p. 84.

[83] PII, p. 93.

[84] PII, p. 118.

[85] PII, p. 231.

[86] PII, p. 231.

[87] PII, p. 236.

[88] PII, pp. 241-42.

[89] PII, p. 245.

[90] Karl Foldenauer, "Hugo von Hofmannsthal und die französische Literatur des 19. und 20. Jahrhunderts" (Diss. Tübingen 1958), pp. 125-131.

[91] PIV, pp. 50-51.

[92] PIV, p. 53.

[93] PIV, p. 142.

[94] PIV, p. 394.

[95] PIV, p. 395.

[96] PIV, p. 402.

[97] PIV, p. 488.

[98] PIV, p. 488.

⁹⁹*PIV*, pp. 488-89.

¹⁰⁰*PIV*, pp. 488-89.

CHAPTER THREE

THE AFFIRMATION OF LIFE

In *The Romantic Agony*, an exhaustive catalogue of the erotic perversions which pervade Romantic and "Decadent" literature, Mario Praz has made some observations which are highly pertinent to our discussion. He writes:

> . . . to such an extent were Beauty and Death looked upon as sisters by the Romantics that they became fused into a sort of two-faced herm, filled with corruption and melancholy and fatal in its beauty -- a beauty of which, the more bitter the taste, the more abundant the enjoyment.[1]

The transition from the Romantic literature of the first half of the nineteenth century to the Decadent writing of the latter half is marked, according to Praz, by the turn from the Fatal Man of Byron's poems and the Gothic novels, who destroys all that he touches, to the Fatal Woman, the cold yet seductive beauty who lures men to their destruction. Although the worship of pure, virginal female beauty which one finds in the Pre-Raphaelites and other artists of Aestheticism seems to form a counter-ideal, this is only apparently the case, for this virginal beauty remained on her pedestal only as long as her sexuality was not brought into play; when this occurred, she appeared in the guise of a vampire or Medusa. In any case, what is notably lacking in virtually all of this literature is any positive acceptance of woman as a flesh-and-blood creature, and thus any relation to the erotic sphere which might be described as life-affirming.

We have seen in the previous chapter that Hofmannsthal was very much aware of these tendencies in the literature of his time, especially in his comparison of the healthy and organic "Liebe zu zweien" of Goethe's <u>Römische Elegien</u> with the "halb wundertätiges Maddonnenbild, halb raffinierte Autosuggestion" which is love in D'Annunzio's work of the same title. In this chapter we shall see how Hofmannsthal, more than any other major writer of his time, sought to escape from this misogynous tendency of the day and create a new image of woman in which human fertility is affirmed, and in which man and woman unite in harmony in the service of life. But this new perspective, as is clear from the previous chapter, has implications far beyond the purely erotic level; the fertility of childbearing is analogous to that of active social involvement, as well as that of artistic creation. Before we turn to Hofmannsthal, though, we must first examine a work which is one of the most famous depictions of the Fatal Woman, a work which towers above almost all others in this tradition in psychological subtlety, to say nothing of artistic quality.

Section One: "Si la beauté n'était la mort . . . .": Mallarmé's "Hérodiade"

The figure of Hérodiade preoccupied Mallarmé for a longer

time than any other; just as it was in the course of his agonizing struggles to create this work in Tournon and Avignon in the 1860s that Mallarmé articulated his own poetics and developed his unique style, it was also "Hérodiade" which preoccupied him at the very end of his life, as evidenced by the bibliography he prepared for the first Pléiade edition of his works, published a year after his death. This is surely an indication of the importance which Mallarmé attached to the poem, and the central position it may well have occupied in the Livre which the poet strove to create.

But as soon as we mention Mallarmé's "Hérodiade," a problem immediately arises: precisely to which texts are we referring? In the Pléiade edition of the Oeuvres Complètes, three segments of the work appear: the "Ouverture Ancienne," a monologue spoken by Hérodiade's nurse, the "Scène," a dialogue between Hérodiade and her nurse, and the "Cantique de Saint Jean," a poem in strophic form spoken by the Baptist at the moment of his decapitation. The "Scène," which was the first in order of composition, was also the only section to be published during the poet's lifetime: it appeared in the Parnasse Contemporain of 1869, and subsequently in 1886 and 1887. By contrast, the "Cantique de Saint Jean" was published only in 1913 and the "Ouverture" in 1926. In 1959, Gardner Davies published an attempted reconstruction of the work as visualized by the poet towards the end of his life, based on sketches and fragments which had not previously appeared, entitled <u>Les noces d'Hérodiade. Mystère.</u>[2] Though these additional texts are of great interest to anyone concerned with the poet's work, their arrangement, as Davies admits, is a result of educated guesswork, and should only be regarded as provisional; in no sense can these texts, some of them fragmentary, be construed to constitute a complete work.

If one wishes to discuss the work "as a whole," then, it is necessary to make an imaginative reconstruction of one's own, to create, using the materials made available by Davies, the missing links between the three sections which appear in the Pléiade edition. Since an undertaking of this kind would lead far beyond the purposes of the present study, I have decided to limit the discussion here to the "Scène." There are several other reasons for this. The "Scène" is the only section of the three in the Pléiade edition which was written while Mallarmé still intended the work for the theater, a plan he had given up by the time he composed the "Ouverture Ancienne." And yet, its repeated publication with only slight revisions during the poet's lifetime, and his inclusion of it as part of the projected work <u>Les noces d'Hérodiade</u> in the last years of his life, indicate clearly that the section had not lost its validity for Mallarmé, despite the shift in generic intention. By contrast, the "Ouverture Ancienne," which was declared by the poet at the time of its composition to be far superior to the "Scène,"[3] was slated to be replaced in the poet's final plan. And yet, it is not only <u>faute de mieux</u>

that we restrict ourselves to the "Scène," for this dramatic poem as we have it is complete in itself; not in terms of the "story," which was not Mallarmé's primary concern, but in terms of its imagery and its revelation of the personality of the heroine. Finally, there is also a more practical reason for the decision: barring the extremely unlikely possibility that Mallarmé had allowed Stefan George to make a hand copy of the unpublished sections which George then transmitted to Hofmannsthal, the "Scène" is the only section which Hofmannsthal could have known in the period including his "lyrical decade," the composition of <u>Elektra</u>, and the conception and initial work on <u>Die Frau ohne Schatten</u>. It is this fact which is decisive in the light of the claim I shall make that Hofmannsthal wrote these two works with "Hérodiade" in mind.

* * *

In the following analysis of the "Scène" from "Hérodiade," it is our intention to follow some of the central imagery of the poem, in an effort to see how it is through this imagery, rather than through actions or direct communication between the characters (as in traditional drama), that the inner state of the heroine is revealed. These are the opening lines of the nurse, addressed to her mistress:

>   Tu vis! ou vois-je ici l'ombre d'une princesse?
>   A mes lèvres tes doigts et leurs bagues et cesse
>   De marcher dans un âge ignoré. . . .

The image of Hérodiade as a shadow recurs three times more during the course of the poem, and its sense is indicated by the context of these lines. The nurse presents an alternative: either Hérodiade is alive, or it is only her shadow that she sees. Clearly, "ombre" is used here in the sense of a ghost, an insubstantial spirit, something that does not partake of human life. This idea of Hérodiade's detachment from the human sphere is further reinforced by the "location" of her wanderings: not in any given place in the present time, but in an "âge ignoré." The role of the nurse emerges clearly in these lines; she tries here, as she will throughout the "Scène," to lure the princess back into the sphere of the human. Her attempt to kiss Hérodiade's hand is only the first of three such "temptations," each of which is rebuffed by her mistress.

Hérodiade's words in reply leave no doubt as to her attitude:

>   Reculez.
> Le blond torrent de mes cheveux immaculés
> Quand il baigne mon corps solitaire le glace
> D'horreur, et mes cheveux que la lumière enlace
> Sont immortels. O femme, un baiser me tûrait
> Si la beauté n'était la mort. . . .

Even the contact with her own hair, which is "immaculate" and "immortal," causes her body to freeze with horror -- how much more horrible, she implies, would be the touch of the nurse's warm lips! This first of several references to her hair is combined with the water imagery which runs throughout the poem: her hair is a "blond torrent" which bathes her body. The nurse's kiss would kill her, she says, "si la beauté n'était la mort . . .," if in her pristine beauty she were not already "dead." In a letter to Villiers de l'Isle-Adam of December 31, 1865, Mallarmé wrote, à propos of "Hérodiade":

> En un mot, le sujet de mon oeuvre est la Beauté, et le sujet apparent n'est qu'un prétexte pour aller vers Elle. C'est, je crois, le mot de la Poésie.[4]

If Hérodiade is an emblem for beauty, this notion of cold, static, and heartless beauty is not new with Mallarmé. It is essentially the same as that of the goddess who speaks in Baudelaire's sonnet "La Beauté":

> Je suis belle, o mortels! comme un rêve de pierre. . . .
> Je hais le mouvement qui déplace les lignes,
> Et jamais je ne pleure et jamais je ne ris.

Clearly this is the ideal towards which Hérodiade aspires. But unlike Baudelaire's serene and implacable goddess, we can see even in these opening lines that Hérodiade feels her immaculate, virginal beauty to be threatened: thus the horror she feels at any human contact, even that of her own "immortal" hair. Her hair is threatening in its watery aspect: water is universally associated with the origins of life, and here it is in motion, a torrent which threatens her static beauty.

In the lines which follow, Hérodiade recalls her entry into the "lourde prison de pierres et de fer" where her lions are kept. The sense of this passage is one of unveiling:

> Je m'arrête rêvant aux exils, et j'effeuille,
> Comme près d'un bassin dont le jet d'eau m'accueille,
> Les pâles lys qui sont en moi, tandis qu'épris
> De suivre du regard les languides débris
> Descendre, à travers ma rêverie, en silence,
> Les lions, de ma robe écartent l'indolence
> Et regardent mes pieds qui calmeraient la mer.

The petals of the lily which she strips away may be taken as a metaphor for her clothes, although the internalization of this flower in the phrase "en moi" seems to undermine this meaning. The reference to the lions who "de ma robe écartent l'indolence" is equally ambiguous. But whether or not in a literal sense, it is clear that she reveals herself to the lions, and this encounter is erotic. It is significant that the "unveiling" takes place by a pool with a fountain which "welcomes" her; the association of water with the forces of life, and by extension the erotic, has already been noted. The lions are caught up in observing her; the word <u>regard</u> appears twice in the passage, and its erotic significance is suggested in Robert de Montesquiou's report of a conversation with the poet,[5] who is said to have told him that the continuation of "Hérodiade" was to depict the sexual "violation" of the princess through the <u>glance</u> of St. John, an offense which could only be rectified by the latter's demise.

Yet if the erotic nature of this encounter suggests a

threat to Hérodiade's virginal self-enclosure, it is still true that she has emerged relatively unscathed; her hands, which are now threatened by the nurse's kiss, remain "sauves." She reveals herself, and yet she is detached and in a dreamy state: "rêvant aux exils," "à travers ma rêverie," "l'indolence." As observed, this erotic encounter is one of sight only; no actual touch is suggested. Later on in the poem, Hérodiade exclaims, in response to her nurse's insistent references to a future lover: "Mais qui me toucherait, des lions respectée?" Thus for Hérodiade the importance of the encounter is that she has emerged untouched. And after all, she has revealed herself, not to a young human lover, but to ancient lions.

She goes on to say to the nurse:

> Calme, toi, les frissons de ta sénile chair,
> Viens et ma chevelure imitant les manières
> Trop farouches qui font votre peur des crinières,
> Aide-moi, puisqu'ainsi tu n'oses plus me voir,
> A me peigner nonchalamment dans un miroir.

Thus, Hérodiade still appears to be confident that she is immune to Eros; it is the nurse whose senile flesh shudders in arousal, though one might view this as a projection onto the nurse of her own feelings. And in this passage she actually seems to identify with the lions (which she had originally called "mes lions"); her hair imitates the manner of the lions' manes, which the nurse fears. Thus the princess, who earlier was implied to be a disembodied spirit, here is shown to be akin to the animal world. And the lions are chosen not only for their connotation of royalty; as is suggested by the adjective "farouche," it is the ferocity of the jungle beast with which it is suggested that Hérodiade has a kinship. This association of the erotic with the ferocious and destructive points ahead to the calamity which awaits her and the Baptist in their encounter, and confirms her to be one of Praz's "Fatal Women."

Hérodiade tells the nurse to assist her in combing her hair in the mirror, since the latter cannot bear to see this "chevelure" in its wild, untamed state. But now the nurse presents the second temptation; she offers her perfume, "Ravie aux vieillesses de roses," for her hair. The progression from the "pâles lys qui sont en moi" to the roses of the perfume is hardly accidental. If lilies are traditionally a symbol of purity, the rose has always been associated with sexual passion, with an additional suggestion of blood and cruelty. The two flowers both appear in the early poem "Les Fleurs," and the name of Hérodiade is associated with the rose:

> L'hyacinthe, le myrte à l'adorable éclair
> Et, pareille à la chair de la femme, la rose
> Cruelle, Hérodiade en fleur du jardin clair,
> Celle qu'un sang farouche et radieux arrose!

In trying to associate herself with the whiteness of the lily, which "ascends dreamily towards the moon," we may surmise that she is suppressing her true nature. Thus the nurse's offer of perfume from roses, especially with the suggestion of sexual violation ("ravie"), provokes a strong reaction:

>Laisse là ces parfums! ne sais-tu
>Que je les hais, nourrice, et veux-tu que je sente
>Leur ivresse noyer ma tête languissante?
>Je veux que mes cheveux qui ne sont pas des fleurs
>A répandre l'oubli des humaines douleurs
>Mais de l'or, à jamais vierge des aromates,
>Dans leurs éclairs cruels et dans leurs pâleurs mates,
>Observent la froideur stérile du métal,
>Vous ayant reflétés, joyaux du mur natal,
>Armes, vases depuis ma solitaire enfance.

She does not want the intoxication of the perfume to "drown" her languid head; just as earlier the "torrent" of her hair horrified her, here again she fears being submerged in this fluid, with its associations of motion and life. In the very revealing passage which follows, she insists on the inorganic nature of her hair. It is not a flower, but made of gold, "à jamais vierge des aromates." Flowers, she suggests, have an intoxicating quality which makes one oblivious to human sorrows. She does not reject the perfume out of compassion for human misery, however; she aspires to the condition of metal with its "cruel lustre." This passage is very revealing psychologically. If in the lions scene her dreamy, languid state was a defense against any overt encounter with her own sexuality, here she shows an awareness of the danger, and rejects the intoxication which would overcome her in her state of defenseless languor. Thus she seizes on the "froideur stérile du métal"; the defensive nature of this choice is further suggested in the reference to the military hardware on the wall of her chamber. In its metallic brilliance, her hair is a mirror which reflects arms and vases, "joyaux du mur natal."

This leads directly into Hérodiade's next speech, the famous apostrophe to the mirror:

> O miroir!
> Eau froide par l'ennui dans ton cadre gelée,
> Que de fois et pendant des heures, désolée
> Des songes et cherchant mes souvenirs qui sont
> Comme des feuilles sous ta glace au trou profond,
> Je m'apparus en toi comme une ombre lointaine,
> Mais, horreur! des soirs, dans ta sévère fontaine,
> J'ai de mon rêve épars connu la nudité!

It is no surprise that the mirror, emblem of narcissistic self-involvement, forms a major image in the poem. What is surprising is that the mirror is here associated with the water imagery we noted earlier: it is cold water which has been frozen by <u>ennui</u>. Thus the vital, dynamic aspects of water which we noted earlier are neutralized; the coldness which surrounds Hérodiade (cf. "froideur stérile du métal" in the preceding speech), and which is an aspect of the boredom suggested in "que de fois et pendant des heures," has caused the water to become hard and static. There is a general sense of entrapment here: Hérodiade seeks her memories which are like dead leaves trapped in an icy lake, she is abandoned by the dreams which might point to a future (owing to the enjambment after <u>désolée</u>, the word has the double meaning of "saddened" and "abandoned," as Szondi has pointed out), and thus she cannot escape the present. Just as the nurse in the opening lines asks rhetorically if it is a shadow she sees, Hérodiade sees herself in the mirror as a distant shadow. If the lions scene was only implicitly a self-revelation, this is explicity so; where her dreaminess earlier was a kind of "defense" against an awareness of her own sexuality, here, in a wonderfully compressed image, she sees the nakedness of her own dream, suggesting at once a physical nakedness and a recognition of her own erotic fantasies and desires.

The physical aspect of this image is confirmed as Hérodiade turns to her nurse to ask if she is beautiful. This encourages the nurse; she replies "un astre, en vérité," but even as she says this she tries to pull Hérodiade down to a human level by attempting to adjust a plait of her hair which has fallen out of place. This is the third "temptation," and it provokes the most violent reaction of all. Her gesture, says Hérodiade, is an impiety, a crime "qui refroidit mon sang vers sa source." Where earlier water froze to form a mirror, here her blood freezes at the prospect of human contact, thus extending the image of "freezing with horror" in her opening lines. These three approaches make up for Hérodiade

> . . . un jour
> Qui ne finira sans malheur sur la tour . . .
> O jour qu'Hérodiade avec effroi regarde!

This is a clear reference to the impending disaster of her

encounter with John the Baptist. Hérodiade, who had up to now appeared to be floating in time, is confronted with the ominous reality of the present day; her entrapment in the present moment parallels her awareness of her own human sexuality, which horrifies her.

By now even the nurse is worried and seeks to soothe her mistress:

> Temps bizarre, en effet, de quoi le ciel vous
>   garde!
> Vous errez, ombre seule et nouvelle fureur,
> Et regardant en vous précoce avec terreur;
> Mais toujours adorable autant qu'une immortelle,
> O mon enfant, et belle affreusement . . .

Once more Hérodiade is called a shadow. Here the savagery which was merely suggested before in the association of Hérodiade with the lions, emerges clearly: she is a "nouvelle fureur," her self-contemplation fills her with terror. The phrase "belle affreusement" recalls once more the "Medusean beauty" of Praz's Fatal Woman. Clearly, the nurse is now aware of the danger inherent in the princess' self-involved beauty and now repeatedly attempts to interest her in a male lover, a suggestion which of course horrifies Hérodiade even more. The nurse asks her for whom she is saving "la splendeur ignorée / Et le mystère vain de votre être?", to which Hérodiade replies: for herself alone. The nurse exclaims: "Triste fleur qui crôit seule et n'a pas d'autre émoi / Que son ombre dans l'eau vue avec atonie." In these brief lines the nurse combines several images encountered previously. Opposing once more her mistress' identification with the metallic and inorganic, she calls her a flower growing alone, and suggests with a hint of mockery that Hérodiade's anxiety has no other cause than the sight of her shadow viewed in reflecting water "avec atonie." The nurse challenges her to explain her triumphant disdain. Hérodiade does not reply directly, but once more expresses her aversion to anything human:

> Du reste, je ne veux rien d'humain et, sculptée,
> Si tu me vois les yeux perdus au paradis
> C'est quand je me souviens de ton lait bu jadis.

She sees herself as a sculpture, recalling once more Baudelaire's stone goddess Beauté. Again she tries to take refuge in dreams, even in memories of childhood. These lines recall the cluster of images associated with l'azur, pointing back to the "seraphic state" identified by Richard in Mallarmé's youthful poetry, and ultimately to the topos of a "vie antérieure" in Baudelaire, all of which were discussed at the beginning of the first chapter. The fond reference to the milk drunk at her nurse's breast illustrates unmistakably the attempt of a girl, emerging into womanhood and frightened by her awakening sexuality, to revert to childhood patterns. If we recall the lines addressed to her mirror, we see the hopelessness of this "escape"; there is a clear opposition between the harmless "rêveries" of the sunlit sky of day, and what is paradoxically the clearer, "severe" vision of night when her dream is revealed in its nakedness, its reality.

The nurse is softened by her mistress' childish recollection and explains in pity "Victime lamentable à son destin offerte!", at which Hérodiade launches into the most extended speech of the "Scène":

> Oui, c'est pour moi, pour moi, que je fleuris, déserte!
> Vous le savez, jardins d'améthyste, enfouis
> Sans fin dans de savants abîmes éblouis,
> Ors ignorés, gardant votre antique lumière
> Sous le sombre sommeil d'une terre première,
> Vous, pierres où mes yeux comme de pures bijoux
> Empruntent leur clarté mélodieuse, et vous
> Métaux qui donnez à ma jeune chevelure
> Une splendeure fatale et sa massive allure!

She accepts the nurse's description of her as a flower blooming only for itself, but then connects the flower image with the domain of the metallic, with which she associates herself more explicitly than before. These "gardens of amethyst," to which Hérodiade appeals as a witness and as a parallel to her own state, are hidden beneath the earth in abysses which are blinded by their brilliance. As Szondi has pointed out, the etymological meaning of amethyst is "resisting intoxication" and the stone was considered a protection against drunkenness, so its appearance here ties in with Hérodiade's rejection of the intoxicating perfumes.[6] She appeals also to undiscovered gold, preserving its ancient lustre beneath the sleep of a primal earth. Both are of course images of metallic radiance which is hidden, the beauty of which is unseen by human eyes -- the condition to which Hérodiade aspires. Referring now to her own immediate environment, she speaks of precious stones which lend her eyes their brilliance, and metals which give her hair "une splendeur fatale et sa massive allure." This line must cause us to take notice. The beauty of metals buried in the earth cannot be alluring, since there is no being for them to attract; similarly, the phrase "splendeur fatale" inevitably suggests the destructive impact of her beauty upon another being. As if recalling this danger, in anger she turns on the nurse,

> . . . selon qui, des calices
> De mes robes, arôme aux farouches délices,
> Sortirait le frisson blanc de ma nudité,
> Prophétise que si le tiède azur d'été,
> Vers lui nativement la femme se dévoile,
> Me voit dans ma pudeur grelottante d'étoile,
> Je meurs!

In this passage, which ties together numerous images we have already encountered, Hérodiade expresses her full horror at the sexual consummation which her nurse wishes for her. The phrase "calices de mes robes" makes explicit what in the lions scene was only suggested, namely the equation of flower petals with her clothing. Where before she had taken refuge in contemplation, "les yeux perdus au paradis," she now takes up the nurse's reference to her as a star, a nocturnal creature who would die if her "pudeur grelottante d'étoile" were exposed to the warm blue summer sky. Knowing that she cannot really be a metal hidden in earth, she nonetheless takes refuge in her own virginity and enforced sterility:

> J'aime l'horreur d'être vierge et je veux
> Vivre parmi l'effroi que me font mes cheveux
> Pour, le soir, retirée en ma couche, reptile
> Inviolé sentir en la chair inutile
> Le froid scintillement de ta pâle clarté
> Toi qui te meurs, toi qui brûles de chasteté,
> Nuit blanche de glaçons et de neige cruelle!
> Et ta soeur solitaire, ô ma soeur éternelle
> Mon rêve montera vers toi: telle déjà,
> Rare limpidité d'un coeur qui le songea,
> Je me crois seule en ma monotone patrie
> Et tout, autour de moi, vit dans l'idolâtrie
> D'un miroir qui reflète en son calme dormant
> Hérodiade au clair regard de diamant. . . .
> O charme dernier, oui! je le sens, je suis seule.

It is paradoxically in this explicit affirmation of her virginity that she also fully accepts her own sexuality for the first time; this apparent contradiction is summed up in the phrase "toi qui brûles de chasteté." She can savor the "scintillement" of her flesh, secure in the knowledge that this flesh is "inutile." She is now fully aware of the frightful, non-human nature of her virginal beauty ("horreur," "effroi," "reptile," "cruelle"). Having rejected the warm light of day, she now turns to the "nuit blanche de glaçons et de neige cruelle" and the moon, its solitary and eternal sister, to which her dream now rises, as it did earlier towards the blue sky of day. It is symptomatic of the greater degree of self-awareness and clarity, "limpidité," which she has achieved here that she speaks explicitly of her environment for the first time, referring to her "monotone patrie." Everything surrounding her becomes an extension of herself, existing in the idolatry of her image reflected in the mirror, a mirror which has now lost its troubled, "watery" aspect and now reflects Hérodiade's "clair regard de diamant." Amid this self-reflecting little world, she senses once more that she is alone.

Her simple-minded nurse has of course understood nothing of this, and seizing on the words "je meurs," asks fearfully "Madame, allez-vous donc mourir?", to which Hérodiade replies:

>   Non, pauvre aïeule,
> Sois calme et, t'éloignant, pardonne à ce coeur
>   dur,
> Mais avant, si tu veux, clos les volets, l'azur
> Séraphique sourit dans les vitres profondes,
> Et je déteste, moi, le bel azur!

There is a stiking change of tone here as she addresses the nurse; no longer cold and contemptuous, there is a sense of calm resignation to her destiny as she gently asks the old woman to leave her. Her request that the shutters be closed confirms her rejection of the light of day and its "rêveries," making explicit its association with the "état séraphique" to which we have referred. For one final moment, she dreams of escape:

>   Des ondes
> Se bercent et, là-bas, sais-tu un pays
> Où le sinistre ciel ait les regards haïs
> De Vénus qui, le soir, brûle dans le feuillage:
> J'y partirais.

The words "sais-tu un pays. . . . J'y partirais" recall that most famous expression of longing for escape into a distant land: Mignon's song from Goethe's <u>Wilhelm Meisters Lehrjahre</u>, "Kennst du das Land." This theme of flight appears repeatedly in Mallarmé's work around this time, in such poems as "Les Fenêtres," "L'Azur," and "Brise Marine." But as in all these cases, such an escape is impossible. Szondi is probably correct in asserting that Hérodiade's later words, "Vous mentez, ô fleur nue / De mes lèvres" refer on the most literal level precisely to this dream of an escape, which she immediately recognizes as a false hope.[7] But the imagery of this sentence points beyond the obvious meaning of lips as the vehicle of words. Lips of course also imply the sensuality of a kiss, a meaning further reinforced by the phrase "fleur nue," which points back to the peeling off of the flower's petals in the lions scene. Hérodiade's final words show her in an attitude of resigned expectation of the "unknown thing" to come:

> J'attends une chose inconnue
> Ou peut-être, ignorant le mystère et vos cris,
> Jetez-vous les sanglots suprêmes et meurtris
> D'une enfance sentant parmi les rêveries
> Se séparer enfin ses froides pierreries.

The unknown event which is to come, the reader can guess, is at least on one level her encounter with John the Baptist, which has been hinted at previously and which is of course part of the reader's expectation from this particular legend. But since we are remaining within the scope of the "Scène," we can read these lines as Hérodiade's final recognition of her emergence into womanhood; the image of the separating rocks implies the crumbling of the protective armor with which she had tried to fend off her own sexuality. The reference to "sanglots" here and "pleurs" a few lines earlier also suggests that she is no longer a stone goddess but a human being, unlike Baudelaire's Beauté who neither laughs nor cries.

*   *   *

If in this reading of the "Scène" I have emphasized the psychological aspect more than is usually done, this was intentional. Many interpreters, in their zeal to view the virginal princess as an emblem of beauty, or of the poet, have overlooked the fact that on its most immediate level the poem is a study of the awakening of a girl into womanhood, portrayed with great psychological insight and acuity. To be sure, this is no conventional psychological drama, for this character development is revealed not in the heroine's actions or her language of communication, but in the imagery of her speeches, which forms an interconnected web of metaphor whose self-reflexivity parallels the heroine's own. And of course it is true, as this last point suggests, that Hérodiade represents the poet who in his attempt to create a pure poetry is haunted by the spectre of sterility, who is constantly reminded of the conflict of this aspiration toward beauty with human frailty and impotence. And yet, in emphasizing this point there is the danger of pulling the poem into the sphere of autobiography. It is well to remember the ironic fact that it was during the composition of "Hérodiade" in November 1864 that Mallarmé's wife gave birth to their first child, an irony of which the poet was fully aware as he wrote to his friend Theodore Aubanel:

> Pour moi, je ne me suis pas encore remis au travail: avec ses cris, ce méchant baby a fait s'enfuir Hérodiade aux cheveux froids comme l'or, aux lourdes robes, stérile.[8]

Thus there is a sharp contrast between the almost hysterical aversion of his heroine towards sexual contact, to say nothing of childbearing, and the more or less normal family life upon which the poet was just then embarking. And yet his choice of a heroine is still revealing, not only of the poet's attitudes towards female sexuality and fertility, but also that of his entire artistic generation, as is so massively documented by Mario Praz. Charles Mauron's generally persuasive attempt to trace Mallarmé's preoccupations to childhood traumas becomes less persuasive when one sees the same preoccupations reflected in the work of his contemporaries.[9] But, as should be apparent from this analysis, Mallarmé's work towers above that of his contemporaries in its enormous poetic achievement, its richness of metaphor, its avoidance of the more lurid aspects of the subject (in contrast, for example, to Wilde's <u>Salomé</u>) and in the subtlety of its character study, which combines sympathy with critical detachment.

Section Two: Hofmannsthal and the Thematics of Fertility

In the second chapter it was seen how Hofmannsthal's critique of Aestheticism is frequently expressed in organic terms: the cult of the inorganic in Aestheticism, with its constant threat of artistic sterility, is opposed to Hofmannsthal's own ideal of engagement in life, of affirmation of the organic and life-giving. It is the purpose of this section to show how these concerns are expressed in two works of Hofmannsthal's maturity, and to view these works in the light of Mallarmé's "Hérodiade."

Whatever may have been Hofmannsthal's early attachment to the art of Aestheticism, and despite the persistence of some critics in labelling the poet a "Decadent," his work from its very beginning is almost wholly free from the misogynous aspects of the Decadent literature surveyed by Praz. The only figures who correspond to the "Fatal Woman" type are the witch in Der Kaiser und die Hexe and, to a lesser degree, the Bergkönigin in Das Bergwerk zu Falun; both of these, however, are non-human and literally demonic figures. A more significant female type in the early work is that of the passive woman, full of dissatisfaction and vague longings, who is swept up into infidelity to her husband or lover almost against her will: Arlette in Gestern, the smith's wife in Idylle, Dianora in Die Frau im Fenster, Sobeide in Die Hochzeit der Sobeide. The passive nature of these figures is almost dictated by the generic nature of the fin-de-siècle lyrical drama as described by Szondi, with its lack of action. These figures correspond in Praz's schema to the victims of the Byronic "Fatal Man" in the Romantic literature of the first half of the century, the most famous of which is Gretchen in Goethe's <u>Faust</u>. If these figures do not represent an especially positive model of feminine character or conduct, they are still far more sympathetic than the innumerable Medusa-like "Fatal Women" of Decadent literature.

And yet as early as 1893, a new kind of female type emerges in Hofmannsthal's works in the figure of Alkestis, in his adaptation of Euripides' drama. These women all are characterized by a capacity for self-sacrifice, though this is not always as absolute as that of Alkestis. They embody a kind of spiritual wholeness and ethical stature almost entirely lacking in his male figures, whether one considers the aesthetes of the lyrical dramas or the rootless adventurers of later works. A few of the better-known examples of this type are Cristina in <u>Cristinas Heimreise</u>, the Marschallin in <u>Der Rosenkavalier</u>, Helene in <u>Der Schwierige</u>, and, as we shall see, the empress in <u>Die Frau ohne Schatten</u>. Neither <u>femmes fatales</u> nor passive victims, these women have a great capacity for love, they are vulnerable, but they possess a degree of self-mastery which enables them to rise above their own personal affections. To all these women could be applied those lines from Goethe's <u>Geheimnisse</u>, which Hofmannsthal quoted in connection with <u>Die Frau ohne Schatten</u>: "Von der Gewalt, die alle Menschen bindet, / Befreit der Mensch sich, der sich überwindet."

Hofmannsthal's depiction of women does not concern us <u>per se</u>, but rather as a further indication of his affirmation of the organic and life-giving. This does not suggest by any means that a woman is defined for Hofmannsthal solely by her childbearing function, nor conversely that the rearing of children is seen as an exclusively female concern. I would suggest, however, that the misogyny of most Decadent writers was deeply symptomatic of their aversion to the organic, to the giving of life, which on a purely biological plane is an exclusively female function, and in this respect the work of Hofmannsthal stands as a sharp and exemplary contrast. For the female figures in Hofmannsthal's mature works are supreme embodiments of an ideal of humanity, and thus in affirming the feminine principle he proclaims this ideal of humanity to an age whose art, to borrow Ortega y Gasset's term, is characterized by dehumanization.

Before we examine <u>Die Frau ohne Schatten</u> as the poet's supreme expression of this ideal, we must first consider a work which presents a world in which no such ideal seems possible, but one in which the thematics of fertility predominate to such an extent that we cannot ignore it here.

A. Elektra

Hofmannsthal wrote his adaptation of Sophocles' Electra during the summer of 1903, and it is thus the first major work he completed following the "Chandos crisis." Since the other work which occupied him during this period was an adaptation of Otway's Venice Preserved, several critics have suggested that the poet was still "recovering" from an artistic sterility he suffered from during this crisis, and was not yet ready to produce a wholly "original" work. One can only assume that these critics have never read Sophocles' play, or at any rate that they have never taken the trouble to compare it with Hofmannsthal's, for the differences between them are so fundamental that there is far more to contrast than to compare.

The cast of characters is roughly the same, the only difference being that there is no Chorus in Hofmannsthal, only individual servants. But this difference represents a fundamental distinction in the moral universe of the two plays. In Sophocles, the Chorus, which bears witness to the injustice of Agamemnon's murder by Clytaemnestra and Aegisthus, represents a continuing moral order which is never really questioned, and which is confirmed in Orestes' just revenge at the conclusion. In Hofmannsthal's play, there is a moral chaos even more fundamental than that at the opening of Aeschylus' Oresteia, which in Aeschylus is replaced at the end of the trilogy by a new moral order achieved through enormous struggle and suffering. The moral chaos in Hofmannsthal's play is absolute and irredeemable; the world portrayed here is one in which hate and oppression are the only ruling forces.

Two important differences in plot serve to reinforce this point. In Sophocles' play, Orestes and his old guardian Paedagogus appear outside the royal palace in the opening scene and lay final plans for their revenge; thus the audience knows from the start that the cleansing of the House of Atreus is at hand, and there is no uncertainty or suspense in this regard. By contrast, Hofmannsthal's play opens with a scene involving a group of maidservants and an overseer. They express hostility and contempt for Elektra, and obviously have no qualms about serving Klytämnestra and Ägisth. When the fifth maidservant, evidently the youngest, expresses admiration for Elektra, she is dragged offstage and cruelly beaten. Even Elektra, despite her obsessive loyalty to her father's memory, cannot be said to represent a moral order in any real sense; her life is ruled entirely by an obsessive hatred, and when Orest's revenge is complete, she performs a wild, Maenadic victory dance and then falls dead, since her life no longer has any meaning. This second deviation from Sophocles further underscores the point that there is no redemption possible for the central figure of this play; unlike the treatment of these myths by both Aeschylus and Sophocles, the idea of political legitimacy and the moral order embodied in the state is absent in Hofmannsthal's version.

The most important common feature between the two plays is

the central conflict between Electra and her sister Chrysothemis, and it is this element which explains the interest for Hofmannsthal of Sophocles' particular treatment of the Electra myth. The problem of fidelity to a dead or lost lover is one which Hofmannsthal treated repeatedly, first in the early lyrical comedy Der weiße Fächer and later in Ariadne auf Naxos. And yet, although Hofmannsthal preserves the basic conflict of one sister (Elektra) who is uncompromising in her devotion to her father's memory and her commitment to revenge, with another (Chrysothemis) who wants to make her peace with the situation as it exists and who desires a normal life, the underlying motivation of the conflict, and thus its significance, is different in the two plays. In Sophocles' Electra, as in his Antigone, their conflict is one between loyalty to an ultimate moral order and obeisance to the political authority of the state. In Hofmannsthal, this conflict is one between Elektra, who has foresworn her womanly nature in her all-consuming hatred (yet who tragically cannot herself perform or even assist in the act of revenge), and Chrysothemis, who desires a normal life of marriage and childbearing.

In Sophocles' play, Electra laments to the Chorus:

> I have awaited [Orestes] always
> sadly, unweariedly,
> till I'm past childbearing, till I am past
>   marriage,
> always to my ruin.[10]

and again:

> I am one wasted in childlessness
> with no loving husband for champion.[11]

In Sophocles, though, this is nothing more than the understandable and justified lament of a woman whose mother and stepfather have abused her and denied her the protection and fulfillment of marriage and childbearing, and it is never suggested that this is the central cause of her bitterness. In Hofmannsthal's play, however, Elektra's thwarted sexuality takes the form of a constant obsession. Before she has even appeared on stage, one of the maidservants tells how Elektra had taunted them with these words: "Eßt Fettes und eßt Süßes / und kriecht zu Bett mit euren Männern."[12] The servants, who know how Elektra is regarded by her parents and thus have no fear of her, counter with "Wenn du hungrig bist . . . so ißt du auch," to which Elektra replies "Ich füttre mir einen Geier auf im Leib."[13] Though she implies that the maids' lives are little different from those of animals, it is made clear throughout the play that it is Elektra who has been degraded to the condition of an animal. The malice of the maidservant's reply does betray at least a half-truth, that Elektra envies them for what she does not have herself. But this is only a half-truth, for Elektra has suppressed her own capacity for love and motherhood to such a degree that she can only be pregnant with hatred, as represented in the image of a vulture which she carries in her womb. Again, the overseer reports:

> Und wenn sie uns mit unsern Kindern sieht
> so schreit sie: nichts kann so verflucht sein,
>   nichts,
> als Kinder, die wir hündisch auf der Treppe
> im Blute glitschend, hier in diesem Haus
> empfangen und geboren haben.[14]

There is some truth to Elektra's words: in a house where a woman has murdered her husband, attempted to murder her son, and abused her daughters, the institution of parenthood has been tainted with blood, and it is almost a sacrilege to give birth to children. But again, her fixation on this particular point (she does not, for instance, specifically reproach the maids for their infidelity to the memory of Agamemnon and his rightful heir Orest) moves her reproach out of the sphere of morally-based judgment into that of psychological obsession.

The theme of marriage and childbearing predominates in the first dialogue between Elektra and Chrysothemis. The latter complains that Elektra's unconcealed hostility toward her parents is the only reason that the two sisters are prevented from leading normal lives, and says:

> Kinder will ich haben,
> bevor mein Leib verwelkt, und wärs ein Bauer,
> dem sie mich geben, Kinder will ich ihm
> gebären und mit meinem Leib sie wärmen
> in kalten Nächten, wenn der Sturm die Hütte
> zusammenschüttelt. . . . Nein, ich bin
> ein Weib und will ein Weiberschicksal.[15]

Her willingness to accept even the humblest social condition rather than forsake marriage and childbearing, to which

Elektra naturally responds with contempt, is translated into the realm of action in the later figure of the empress in Die Frau ohne Schatten. But if the conduct of this character is portrayed as exemplary in the latter work, in the case of Elektra, there is no clear indication that Chrysothemis' position is preferable to Elektra's, reflecting a certain ambivalence in the poet at the time of this 1903 work.

For Elektra, the sexual act is inextricably connected with the thought of her mother's relationship with Ägisth, and she scolds her sister for her desires:

>   Pfui,
> die's denkt, pfui, die's mit Namen nennt! Die Höhle
> zu sein, drin nach dem Mord dem Mörder wohl ist;
> das Tier zu spielen, das dem schlimmern Tier
> Ergetzung bietet. Ah, mit einem schläft sie,
> preßt ihre Brüste ihm auf beide Augen
> und winkt dem zweiten, der mit Netz und Beil
> hervorkriecht hinterm Bett.[16]

Chrysothemis calls her "entsetzlich," and wishes to forget "daß es so etwas Grauenvolles gibt," for "das Fürchterliche ist nicht für das Herz der Menschen."[17] Thus Elektra, in her association of the sexual act with murder, terror, and blood, seems at first glance to be a perfect example of Praz's Fatal Woman. And yet this is not really the case, for Elektra is not a destroyer, but rather a victim; it is the central irony of her predicament that she cannot act, cannot even assist (as does Sophocles' Electra) in the act of revenge which is the one hope of her life. It is Elektra's mother

Klytämnestra who has actually participated in the act of murder, and yet in this play she appears as even less of an actual "destroyer" than Elektra. Though weighted down with the tell-tale precious stones with which she hopes to ward off evil omens, she is reduced to a state of near collapse by nightmares foretelling the return of Orest and her own death; if she once was a Fatal Woman, she now appears as a pitiful figure who is hardly less a victim than Elektra herself. Elektra taunts her mother with these words:

> . . . du liegst in deinem Selbst so
>   eingekerkert,
> als wärs der glühende Bauch von einem Tier von
>   Erz . . .[18]

This striking image of imprisonment within the self, with even a suggestion of being pregnant with one's own self, expresses the situation of the aesthete in extremis, and is no less applicable to Elektra herself than to her mother. They are both to such a degree the prisoners of their predicaments that they cannot escape from their own selves into any meaningful contact with another person, and the sterility of this situation is underlined in the image of a bronze animal.

    I could go on to cite numerous passages in the same vein, but by now it should be sufficiently clear that this play is dominated by imagery related to the problems of childlessness versus parenthood, fertility versus sterility, the inorganic versus the organic, a complex of imagery which we saw in

Hofmannsthal's essays as a response to the obsession with the sterile and inorganic in the literature of his contemporaries. But although we have thus established a thematic link between this work and Mallarmé's "Hérodiade," I suggested earlier that there was a more specific link between the two works. This link can be demonstrated in a passage towards the end of the play in which Elektra, having finally been reunited with Orest, tries to excuse her unsightly appearance:

> Ich bin nur mehr der Leichnam deiner Schwester,
> mein armes Kind. Ich weiß, es schaudert dich
> vor mir. Und war doch eines Königs Tochter!
> Ich glaube, ich war schön: wenn ich die Lampe
> ausblies vor meinem Spiegel, wie mein nackter
>   Leib
> vor Unberührtheit durch die schwüle Nacht
> wie etwas Göttliches hinleuchtete.
> Ich fühlte, wie der dünne Strahl des Monds
> in seiner weißen Nacktheit badete
> so wie in einem Weiher, und mein Haar
> war solches Haar, vor dem die Männer
>   zittern. . . .[19]

There is hardly an image in these lines which does not have its exact parallel in "Hérodiade": the mirror in which the princess contemplates her naked body which glows in its "Unberührtheit" and suggests a goddess, the moonbeams which bathe her white nakedness as if in a pool, the hair whose beauty causes others to tremble with fear. So exact is the equivalence that one is led to assume that Hofmannsthal is here consciously and deliberately equating Hérodiade's state with that of the young Elektra. And this insight casts an entirely new light on the character of Elektra. Her entrapment within the self, and the sexual obsession which is related to this, cannot in the light of this passage be explained only as a result of the trauma of her father's murder. In the narcissistic self-contemplation of the young princess, in the glorification of her own <u>Unberührtheit</u>, she already displayed the alienation from normal human involvement which characterizes the Elektra we see on stage. Just as Hérodiade seems to oscillate between goddess and animal while avoiding, until the end of the "Scène," any human aspect, so the princess Elektra, who has been torn by events from her goddess-like state, debases herself into the condition of an animal. The parallel between the two figures appears even closer when one considers that Hérodiade, at least as she appears in the "Scène," seems as incapable of any effective action as Elektra, and is thus equally trapped in her own predicament.

Thus in spite of the obvious differences in their circumstances, there is no denying the kinship between these two figures, and by extension between the two works in which they appear. In each case, the poet views his central figure with a certain amount of sympathy but with a greater amount of critical detachment. And yet, in neither work is an alternative offered, a counter-example of a fully integrated humanity. The insipid and uncomprehending nurse of Hérodiade, although "human" in a not overly positive sense, hardly represents a viewpoint which adequately responds to her mistress' problematic state. Hofmannsthal's Chrysothemis is a more sympathetic and fully realized character, but she cannot be said to represent any ideal of humanity; Elektra points out with some justice that her sister's frantic desire to forget her father's death is a trait more animal than human.

Thus in this play there does not appear one of those female figures referred to earlier who embody an ideal of humanity and self-mastery. There is an interesting fact to be noted in this connection, however. An obvious prototype for this series of female characters in Hofmannsthal's work (Alkestis, Cristina, the Marschallin, the empress) is clearly Goethe's Iphigenie. But in a diary entry of July 17, 1904, in which Hofmannsthal discusses his original conception of Elektra, he specifically opposes his work to Goethe's play:

> Als Stil schwebte mir vor, etwas Gegensätzliches zur "Iphigenie" zu machen, etwas worauf das Wort nicht passe: "dieses gräcisierende Produkt erschien mir beim erneuten Lesen verteufelt human." (Goethe an Schiller)[20]

One need hardly add that he succeeded; it would be difficult to imagine a sharper contrast than that between the atmosphere of Goethe's play and that of Hofmannsthal, between the serene self-mastery of Goethe's heroine and the obsessive, fragmented personality of Hofmannsthal's Elektra. As to the reasons why Hofmannsthal consciously chose to avoid the humanistic atmosphere of Goethe's play, and of his own later work, one can only speculate. Perhaps the memory of his own experience of artistic sterility was too fresh in his mind for him to formulate a positive solution, a way out of the sterile self-enclosure which defines Elektra as it does Hérodiade; the fact remains that in this play Hofmannsthal offers no more of a solution than did Mallarmé in the "Scène" from "Hérodiade."

B. Die Frau ohne Schatten

The years between 1903 and 1911, between the completion of Elektra and the first plan for Die Frau ohne Schatten, were productive and eventful ones for the poet. They witnessed the completion of the other two "Griechendramen" Ödipus und die Sphinx and König Ödipus, the comedies Silvia im "Stern" and Cristinas Heimreise, the success of his first two operatic collaborations with Richard Strauss, Elektra and Der Rosenkavalier, the story "Lucidor," the lecture "Der Dichter und diese Zeit," and several major essays. In spite of the widespread disappointment and incomprehension among his former admirers occasioned by his turn to new forms, and especially the collaboration with Strauss, his poetic rank had been publicly confirmed in 1903 by the publication of Ausgewählte Gedichte by George's "Verlag der Blätter für die Kunst," and in 1907 by the two-volume edition of his collected poems and lyric dramas, and by the publication in the same year of the first two volumes of his prose works. Thus although he had not entirely banished the demon of artistic sterility -- in a 1917 diary entry he quotes Claudel on the empty white spaces of the page which make up a poem, and comments "Hier ist jene

Vorstellung des Leeren, die mich verfolgt"[21] -- one may surmise that he had achieved a certain amount of confidence in his chosen new forms, and thus it is not until the second version of <u>Der Turm</u> in 1927 that we find a work so utterly dominated by the powers of darkness as was <u>Elektra</u>.

When one speaks of <u>Die Frau ohne Schatten</u>, of course, one is speaking not of one but of two complete works: the libretto to Strauss' opera and the prose version which Hofmannsthal wrote at around the same time. I have chosen to deal primarily with the prose version, though I will not hesitate to refer on occasion to the libretto as well. This decision is based not on a judgment of the artistic superiority of one version to another, but on the greater elaboration of character and imagery in the prose version.[22] For the purpose of the present discussion, I will provide a rough outline of the plot, which to the extent possible gives the essential action common to both versions.

The daughter of the spirit-king Keikobad is captured in the form of a gazelle by the emperor of the Southeast Islands, who is out on a hunt. With the wings of his falcon beating down on her head, the emperor is about to kill his prey when a beautiful female emerges from the gazelle (she has the power to transform herself at will). They instantly fall in love and are soon married, but Keikobad has laid a curse on them: if within the space of twelve months the empress does not cast a shadow, which is explicitly an emblem of motherhood ("dies ist ein und dasselbe, Zeichen und Bezeichnetes" wrote Hofmannsthal in his summary of the opera),[23] the emperor must turn to stone. Twelve months have now gone by, each day following the same pattern: the emperor and empress spend their nights together, but the emperor spends all his days hunting. The nurse, who has accompanied the empress from the spirit world, is visited at the beginning of the work by the twelfth of the spirit messengers who have come every month to ask whether the empress casts a shadow. The nurse, who hates the emperor as she does all human beings, can report with satisfaction that she does not. The messenger announces the fulfillment of the curse if she does not acquire a shadow in three days' time. The empress, who had been ignorant of the curse, learns about it now, and, determined to save her husband, she commands the reluctant nurse to assist her in obtaining a shadow in the world of men. They descend to the most populous city in the emperor's realm, where the nurse's diabolical instincts lead them to the hut of Barak the Dyer and his wife. This couple is descended directly from the smith and his wife in "Idylle": he is a simple and unimaginative handworker, she a much younger woman, dissatisfied with her marriage, who yearns for a different life. And yet a comparison of the two couples is most revealing of the way in which Hofmannsthal in his maturity was able to resolve the ambivalence of the early work. In "Idylle" there is an unresolved tension between the wife's aesthetic sense, which prompts her to seek refuge in fantasies, and the real world represented by her husband, the world of duty and hard work, which seems lacking in imagination and beauty. We see the smith's wife crushed by the grim forces of reality, much as the heroes of some of Thomas Mann's early stories, but the poet's ambivalence is reflected in the absence of any clear indication that the point of view of either character is more correct. In the libretto, by contrast, Barak the dyer is clearly the more sympathetic character; his goodness and generosity stand in contrast to his wife's coldness and vanity. (In the opera, this is accented by the evident sympathy of the composer for Barak.) A careful reading of the prose version, however, reveals that the poet's treatment of these characters is not so one-sided.[24] Barak embodies the positive ethical values associated in this work with the continuity and preservation of life through marriage and childbearing. He is a good-natured and cheerful provider for his wife, as well as his three misshapen brothers and even poor children on the street. Above all, he is the "Vorkämpfer der Ungeborenen," and in his fervent desire for parenthood his striving is parallel to that of the empress. Barak's wife seems unsympathetic at first because of her coldness, but it becomes clear that she simply represents a different set of values: just as her husband represents ethical values, she represents the aesthetic sense that is totally lacking in her well-meaning but crude husband. Just as there is a parallel between Barak and the empress in their commitment to the "ethical" values of the work, so there is between the emperor and the dyer's wife, who in their "aestheticism" turn their backs on the claims of life; the emperor's petrifaction is of course a perfect symbol for the predicament of the aesthete who, in trying to preserve a moment or a being of perfect beauty by isolating it from life or change, himself becomes divorced from life.

To return to the story: the nurse is able to entice Barak's wife, during a series of visits, with promises of service, riches, eternal youth, and a handsome young admirer, into parting with her shadow and thus accepting eternal childlessness. Though in both versions it is suggested that the pact has not been fully sealed, she still loses her shadow, and when Barak realizes what has happened he breaks into an unaccustomed rage and threatens to kill her. At this moment, their eyes meet and their true selves are revealed to each other for the first time; they both soften, he in forgiveness for her action and remorse for his threat, she in love and remorse. They are both magically transported into the realm of Keikobad, where the empress and the nurse follow them.

In the meantime, the three days have expired and the emperor enters into a mountain cave in Keikobad's realm and is transformed into a stone statue, as is suggested in a dream of the empress in the libretto and in the central chapter of the prose version. The final section in Keikobad's realm has numerous divergences between the two versions in its complex symbolic landscape, but in both versions the essential events are the same. Barak and his wife, who have found each other in spirit, are separated by physical barriers, and she is still shadowless. The nurse, whose diabolical nature is now apparent, is punished and disappears from the action. The empress is led into the cave where she confronts the stone statue of her husband, and is told that she has but to drink from the Golden Water of Life which flows there, and the shadow of Barak's wife will be hers, and her husband redeemed. But the empress, who has become deeply involved in the lives of the other couple and realizes her own guilt, refuses to drink. By her act of self-mastery she gains a shadow of her own, the shadow of Barak's wife returns to its rightful owner, and the emperor returns to human form. Both couples are joined by a chorus of unborn children in a joyful conclusion. And of course the reuniting of the two couples symbolizes the reconciliation of the ethical and the aesthetic, the claims of life and of beauty.

Even this bare outline immediately suggests several points of contact with "Hérodiade," most obviously the shadow motif. This image forms the basis of the only previous comparison of the two works, an article by F. C. St. Aubyn.[25] St. Aubyn compares the crisis which Mallarmé underwent in Tournon during the composition of the "Scène" from "Hérodiade" with Hofmannsthal's "Chandoskrise," but then goes on to assume a fundamental rejection of Symbolist aesthetics in Hofmannsthal's later work, an assumption which is highly questionable both in the light of Hofmannsthal's post-Chandos essays, and of the analysis of this work which follows. St. Aubyn does not concern himself with the question of influence, and thus he cites parallels with the "Ouverture Ancienne," which Hofmannsthal almost certainly did not know when he wrote <u>Die Frau ohne Schatten</u>, as well as with the "Scène," which Hofmannsthal not only knew but which was very much on his mind as he wrote <u>Elektra</u> and <u>Die Frau ohne Schatten</u>. The use of the shadow image in the two works, as St. Aubyn points out, is antithetical. In Mallarmé's poem, the shadow, which is actually one of the least ambiguous images of the work, suggests Hérodiade's spectral state, with implications both of death and of spirithood, non-humanity. In Hofmannsthal it is not <u>being</u> a shadow but rather <u>having</u> a shadow which is at issue: the shadow represents the ability to give birth and, by extension, full membership in the human race. These two uses of the shadow motif correspond to the two main folkloric traditions involving the motif: the shadow as the only visible sign of incorporeal spirits, and the shadow as the essential sign of motherhood and more generally of belonging to the human community, exactly as it appears in Hofmannsthal.[26] The shadow motif is used in this second sense in Chamisso's famous <u>Peter Schlemihls wundersame Geschichte</u>, a work with which Hofmannsthal was familiar.[27] A more relevant source for Hofmannsthal is the Austrian poet Lenau's "Anna," a version of the

Swedish legend described by Antti Arne and Stith Thompson in The Types of the Folktale.[28] Anna appears at the beginning of the poem contemplating her image in a pond, and is approached by a witch-like figure who promises eternal youth and beauty if she will give up her shadow and renounce childbearing. This narcissistic motif, so reminiscent of Hérodiade, is related to no other motive than vanity: the witch persuades her to renounce childbearing by telling her that it will disfigure her perfect beauty. By contrast, both Hérodiade and Barak's wife are more concerned with preserving their own spiritual and physical Unberührtheit than with merely preserving their physical beauty, though this consideration is present as well.

It will be noticed that in comparing Mallarmé's poem to Die Frau ohne Schatten, Hérodiade has been compared to two different figures: the empress and Barak's wife (hereinafter referred to by the less cumbersome German word Färberin). This is no accident; for just as Hérodiade views her own spectral image in the mirror, the empress sees in the human form of the Färberin a "mirror-image" of herself, a woman whose striving is in some ways parallel and in others antithetical to her own.

First, let us examine the figure of the empress. At the beginning of the work she is associated, as was Hérodiade, with stones and jewels. The nurse tells the spirit messenger:

> So wenig wirft sie Schatten, als ob ihr Leib
> von Bergkristall war. Ja, was sie hinter sich
> läßt, Steine, Rasen, oder Wasser, leuchtet
> nachher stärker auf, so als wäre es Smaragden
> und Topas.29

Just as Hérodiade was implied to be part spirit and part animal at the beginning of the "Scène," the same ambivalence characterizes the empress. She is born a spirit, and her shadowlessness shows that she has not yet cast off her spirit nature. As a spirit, though, she has the ability to transform herself into the forms of various animals. This aspect of her character is further emphasized in her first descent into the human city:

> Das Fürchterliche in den Gesichtern der Menschen
> traf sie aus solcher Nähe wie noch nie. . . . Die
> erbarmungslosen, gierigen und dabei, wie ihr
> vorkam, angstvollen Blicke aus so vielen
> Gesichtern vereinigten sich in ihrer Brust. . . .
> Auf einmal war sie vor den Hufen eines großen
> Maulesels, der wissende, sanfte Blick des Tiers
> traf sie, sie erholte sich an ihm.30

Profoundly alienated by the faces of men, she feels an immediate kinship with the first animal she sees. At this stage, she is only concerned with finding a shadow to save her husband, and she willingly goes along with her nurse's stratagems. Yet in the course of visits to Barak's house, she becomes more and more caught up in the affairs of this human couple, she is increasingly aware of her guilt for their misfortunes, and the example of Barak has presented her with an ideal of humanity which she must strive to achieve. Thus although she does not resist human nature as explicitly as Hérodiade, her becoming human is a process of which she becomes aware only gradually, as does Hérodiade; in both cases the shedding of tears is an essential sign of this process. When the nurse has slipped Barak a sleeping potion to facilitate a visit by the Färberin's secret admirer (actually a malign spirit under the nurse's command), the nurse makes a shocking discovery:

> . . . mit sprachlosen Staunen sah die Amme, daß [der Kaiserin] Wasser aus beiden Augen schoß, daß ihr Gesicht in Schmerz und Tränen schwamm, wie das einer sterblichen Frau.[31]

Of course Hérodiade's "humanization" is predetermined by the fact that she *is*, after all, a human being, and not a star, a goddess, or an animal. But Hofmannsthal suggests that the empress' evolution toward humanity is equally predetermined. Paradoxically, it is her power of transformation, part of her heritage from her spirit father, which enables her to take on animal shapes, and which she loses in marrying a human being, it is this same power which has from the beginning bound her to the realm of humanity. The nurse complains to the twelfth spirit-messenger: "Warum hat er [Keikobad] ihr die Gabe der Verwandlung gegeben? So war sie ja schon den Menschen verfallen!"[32] This idea of transformation, which is central to the work, is seen throughout as an essentially human quality.

The most obvious parallel between the empress and Hérodiade is in their coupling with the figure of a nurse. The relationship of the two to their nurses seems to reflect a deliberate reversal. If Hérodiade's Nourrice fears and distrusts the non-human aspects of her mistress and seeks to win her over to the sphere of normal human desires, the Amme is antagonistic to the "human" qualities of her mistress, and tries to preserve her from human contact. And yet the contrast is not all that absolute. In the libretto the Amme says of human beings: "Betrug ist die Speise, nach der sie gieren, Betrüger sie selber."[33] But it is the Amme herself who is the practitioner of deception in the work, and thus in spite of her spirit origins she seems to represent the baser aspects of humanity. This is confirmed by the words of the Färberin, who says to her ". . . ich verachte dich, das merke dir, und hasse das Niedrige in mir, das mit dir zu tun hat."[34] Seen in this light, there is a degree of similarity between the two nurses: they both embody humanity in its basest form. On the other hand, there is a distinction in what constitutes the baseness of these two figures, one which is characteristic of the opposite values embodied in the two works: the Nourrice is base in her vulgar lasciviousness, her belief that all Hérodiade needs is a male lover, her incomprehension of her mistress' striving towards a state of metallic perfection, and the Amme in her embodiment of human cruelty and deceptiveness, and in her incomprehension of her mistress' human strivings.

Let us turn now to the figure of the Färberin. Several factors suggest that she does in fact represent a kind of mirror-image of the empress. Neither figure's physical appearance is described in any great detail, but one feature is ascribed to both: reference is made to the "Schöne schmale Hüften"[35] of the empress, and the Färberin feels the "Schlankheit ihrer [eignen] Hüften"[36] with her hands. It is no accident that this is a trait associated with virginity; though neither woman is a virgin in the literal sense, they both have preserved a kind of spiritual "Unberührtheit," the Färberin in the unwillingness with which she receives her husband's embraces, the empress in her half-belonging to the spirit world, which implies that her marriage to a mortal cannot have been fully "consummated." This fact is of course underlined by the childlessness of both women. When the empress first sees the Färberin, she finds her "böse und gemein," but this repulsion is gradually replaced by a sense of identification with her. When the nurse has conjured up the Efrit, the spirit who takes on the form of a secret admirer of the Färberin, the empress clearly identifies with that part of her which resisted the spirit's advances. She silently wishes for Barak to come home, and the more helpless the Färberin becomes, the more resolute the empress:

> Der Efrit hatte die Färberin um die Mitte gefaßt: er wollte sie mit sich fortziehen, es schien, als söge er mit der Gefahr einen doppelten frechen Mut in sich. Er war bereit,

> seine Beute hoch in der Luft über den Köpfen
> der Eindringenden hinwegzutragen, und er war
> schön in seiner knirschenden Ungeduld. Die
> Kaiserin trat ihm in den Weg. Ihr Mut war dem
> seinen gleich, sie legte beide Arme um die
> Frau, der Efrit wandte ihr sein Gesicht zu, das
> loderte wie ein offenes Feuer; durch seine zwei
> ungleichen Augen grinsten die Abgründe des nie
> zu betretenden herein, ein Grausen faßte sie,
> nicht für sich selber, sondern in der Seele der
> Färberin, daß diese in den Armen eines solchen
> Dämons liegen und ihren Atem mit dem seinem
> vermischen sollte. Sie wollte die Färberin an
> sich ziehen, sie achtete es nicht, daß es ein
> menschliches Wesen war, um das sie zum ersten
> Male ihre Arme schlang.[37]

It is during the next visit of the empress and the nurse to Barak's house that the Färberin begins to display an intense hostility towards the empress. This can only be explained by the fact that just as the nurse represents to her what is basest in herself, the empress represents her conscience, and her silent presence seems a reproach. It is the empress who helps Barak with his chores, it is she who learns to love the simple dyer -- thus she has in effect assumed the role which rightfully belongs to the Färberin, just as the nurse hopes to gain for her the shadow which is rightfully that of the other woman.

If it is true, as we have seen, that the Färberin is in a sense the empress' mirror-image, it is also the Färberin who specifically echoes the narcissism of Hérodiade. Before the arrival of the empress and the nurse she has no mirror, and the only thing which causes her to smile is feeling the slenderness of her hips with her hands. The nurse, sensing the surest path to ensnare the woman, conjures up a hairband set with jewels and a mirror, in which the Färberin gazes at herself with the new ornament. There is a further, apparently deliberate parallelism between Hérodiade and the Färberin. Just as Hérodiade's nurse offers her three "temptations" to lure her into the human sphere, so the nurse, accompanied by the empress, pays three visits to the dyer's house, each one a renewed temptation for the Färberin. On the first visit, the nurse tells her of a secret admirer, offers to serve her as if she were a princess, and offers her riches and eternal beauty if she will foreswear childbearing. On the second visit, they perform the services of maids for her, and the nurse actually conjures up her admirer. The second temptation of Hérodiade, it will be remembered, was the offer of perfume "ravie aux vieillesses de roses"; in rejecting this, she refers to "mes cheveux qui ne sont pas des fleurs a répandre l'oubli des humaines douleurs." During the second visit, when the Färberin breaks into tears, the nurse tries to soothe her with a scent, to which she replies: "Warum zündest du Weihrauch an, ich will es nicht."[38] Like Hérodiade, she does not wish to be distracted by scents from an awareness of her condition. During the third visit, the nurse drugs Barak to enable his wife to meet once more with her admirer, but this provokes a violent reaction from her.

A comparison of these "temptations" suggests a crucial distinction. Hérodiade sharply rejects all three of her nurse's approaches in an ever-increasing horror of human contact. The Färberin, however, though she ultimately stops short of succumbing entirely, is torn by an inner conflict throughout, and she is obviously tempted by the thought of a lover. But her desire is not essentially a physical one:

> Von diesem Augenblick an war für die schöne Färberin nichts so unumstößlich, als daß sie einen verborgenen Freund von wunderbarer Zartheit des Denkens und Fühlens besitze: das schien ihr vor allem köstlich, daß er von ihrem Dasein bis ins einzelne wußte, über ihr wachte und die Betrübnisse und Kränkungen, an denen ihr junges Leben vermeintlich reich war, mit ihr teilte. . . .[39]

What she longs for is a delicacy of feeling that her loving but coarse husband lacks; she desires to be freed from constant reminders of her lowly condition -- e.g., Barak's three brothers -- and to be treated in a manner befitting her more delicate sensibilities. Before she has seen the Efrit, she imagines him as old and ugly:

> . . . ich will den nicht sehen, der dich ausgeschickt hat; denn ich bin seiner überdrüssig, bevor ich ihn gesehen habe. Die Begehrlichen sind einander gleich auf dieser Welt, und ihr Begehren ekelt mir.[40]

It is the beauty of this apparition that tempts her, in contrast to the physical ugliness of her surroundings. And yet, there is something in her which resists this attraction -- it is her own sense of belonging to her husband, much as she seeks to deny this: "Barak, mein Mann, soll sich freuen, daß ich zwei Dienerinnen habe."[41] Offended at the thought of an ugly old man who desires her, she threatens:

> Erzähle ihm ein wenig, daß Barak der stärkste unter den Färbern ist und auch unter den Lastträgern nicht seinesgleichen hat.[42]

It is when the nurse has drugged her husband with a sleeping potion that she feels the full strength of her ties to him, although she still resents them and feels them as a bondage:

> Wehe . . ., werde ich das Korn sein, wird er das Huhn sein und mich aufpicken! Werde ich das Feuer sein, wird er das Wasser sein und mich auslöschen! Denn ich bin an ihn gekettet mit eisernen Ketten.[43]

This image of chains will undergo a significant transformation during the course of the work, as we shall see later. It is in the scene when her long-patient husband finally rises up in anger to threaten her that her feelings are released:

> Sie sah seinen mächtigen Leib vor sich und die gewaltigen Kräfte, die in ihn eingesperrt waren und aus den Augen, aus dem Mund und den beweglichen Gliedern hervorbrechen wollten, und weil sie dieses Mal nicht begehrend auf sie einstürmten wie ein Bergsturz, so war sie entzaubert und sah ihn mit einem durchdringenden Blick: seine Gewalt war ihr wie eines Löwen und seine Ohnmacht wie eines Kindes; sie erschrak über den ungeheuren Zwiespalt mit einem süßen Schrecken und öffnete sich ganz, diese Zweiheit in sich zu vereinen.[44]

The beauty of the Efrit has awakened her senses, but contrary to the nurse's intention, this only leads her finally to yield to the love of her husband, which she had resisted.

Thus we have seen that the characters of the empress and the Färberin are complementary, and in their dual aspect they form a clear and deliberate parallel to Mallarmé's Hérodiade. The empress in her spirit/animal duality, her alienation from the human sphere, and her relation to her nurse, the Färberin in her narcissism and her instinctive aversion to physical contact, both reflect traits of Mallarmé's virginal princess just as clearly as the young Elektra in the speech quoted earlier. And yet one cannot escape the conclusion that Hofmannsthal has created this parallelism only to stand it on its head. Where for Hérodiade sexuality is inescapably connected with blood, horror, and ultimately death, the empress and the Färberin come to understand their sexuality as part of an organic process, the continuity of human life represented by the omnipresent unborn children. Where for Hérodiade womanhood and humanization are a process of dissolution with untold and dire consequences, for the women in Hofmannsthal's work the attainment of womanhood is a process of integration -- the achievement of personal wholeness within themselves, and the establishment of their place within the human community.

And yet it is not true that Symbolist elements are brought into the work only to be negated. If Hofmannsthal broke with the Symbolist heritage in his affirmative view of the processes of life, his work continues to show a deep indebtedness to Symbolist aesthetics, most specifically in his use of imagery and its function in the work as a whole. To illustrate this point let us examine a cluster of images of central importance to both "Hérodiade" and <u>Die Frau ohne Schatten</u>: those related to water. In "Hérodiade," water appears in a number of guises: the blond "torrent" of the princess' hair which bathes her body, a pool whose fountain greets her in the lions' scene, the liquid perfumes which she rejects because they would drown her languid head, the mirror which is water frozen over by ennui, the white night of icicles and snow, and finally the tears which mark the crumbling of her virginal state. These water images in their various transformations convey the inner progression of the poem. At the beginning she is threatened by the "torrent" of her hair and the vitality suggested by its motion; she retreats to the memory of the lions and the more static pool associated with them, the stasis of which reflects the <u>Unberührtheit</u> she preserves in this encounter; the frozen water of the mirror, the icicles, and the glaciers suggest her attempt to take refuge in the realm of the cold, nocturnal, and inorganic; finally the tears at the end suggest a melting of this ice and of her own personality, particularly in conjunction with the order she gives her nurse to light the torches:

> Allume encore, enfantillage
> Dis-tu, ces flambeaux où la cire au feu léger
> Pleure parmi l'or vain quelque pleur
>   étranger. . . .

Thus the water images in Mallarmé's poems illustrate the kind of metaphoric structure which, as was seen in the first chapter, constitutes one of the most important contributions of French Symbolism to Hofmannsthal's poetic technique.

We can see this same metaphoric structure in the water imagery of <u>Die Frau ohne Schatten</u>. In her youth the empress lived with her nurse on an island in the middle of a lake of ebony-black water, surrounded by the seven "Mondberge" of Keikobad's domain. The blackness and stasis of the lake suggest the timeless, inorganic nature of the spirit world. Similarly, there is a large pool in front of the emperor's Blue Palace, which reflects the coming of the twelfth spirit-messenger; its stasis represents the timeless condition in which both the emperor and the nurse (their desires converge in this one point) try to maintain the empress. But these "still waters" are soon opposed to waters of a different kind: the Golden Water of Life, which is mentioned throughout the work, and which plays a crucial role in the final scene. The twelfth spirit-messenger warns the nurse:

> Nimm dich zusammen und wache über ihr mit hundert Augen. Das goldene Wasser ist auf der Wanderschaft, es wäre nicht gut, wenn sie ihm begegnete.[45]

It is clear that this water poses a threat to the empress' spirithood; the reason for this is given in the final chapter by the fisherman, one of the spirit-messengers, who tells his wife, "das goldene Wasser verwandelt das Unsichtbare." This water is a deeply ambiguous element; explicitly connected with life, its "golden" quality implicitly suggests the inorganic, and it is found in the cave where the stone statue of the emperor sits. In its magical qualities it has the power to gain the Färberin's shadow for the empress, and thus to redeem the emperor from his curse. But the empress rejects this "magical" path and refuses to drink the water, and it is this act of human renunciation which redeems not only her husband, but Barak and his wife as well.

There are several rivers mentioned in the work, which tend to suggest an interconnection of the three realms: that of the spirit world, that of the emperor's palace and his hunting grounds, and that of the city where Barak lives. The river which runs immediately behind the dyer's house, and in which he does his work, is yellow from the dyes which spill into it. This yellow is in one sense a pale, muddy version of the metallic brilliance of the Golden Water of Life. But the dye represents a connection with the world of living things. Barak tells his imaginary children:

> Wir nehmen die Farben aus den Blumen heraus und heften sie auf die Tücher, so auch aus den Würmen, und von den Brüsten der Vögel dort, wo ihre Federn leuchtend und unbedeckt sind.[46]

Thus this water is a perfect emblem for the human world of the city, the apparent ugliness of which conceals a living beauty.

As in "Hérodiade," tears form a part of the water imagery.

At the end of the first chapter, the empress weeps "eine kristallene Träne,"[47] showing her essential spirithood. It is only after her involvement with the human destinies of Barak and his wife that she is able to weep warm, human tears, as we noted earlier.

In the sixth chapter, as the fate of the dyer couple approaches catastrophe, the water imagery is joined by an equally predominant strain of images connected with fire. When Barak first has an inkling of what his wife is about to do, he commands his brothers to build a fire; he has "rotglühenden Augen." The brothers light torches so that they can follow their fleeing sister-in-law in the darkness caused by a storm. It is significant that the Färberin insists on performing her "Unfruchtbarkeitszauber" with fire, rather than flowing water, as the nurse had suggested. This implies that the warmth of fire is a kind of antidote to the dangerous coldness of water (cf. the icicles and glacier of "Hérodiade"); it is fire that the Färberin chooses in her unconscious resistance to her conscious purpose. But fire, as suggested by Barak's glowing eyes and her missing shadow, is also connected with the idea of seeing, which becomes crucial as Barak and his wife are transformed at the end of the chapter when they "see" each other's real selves for the first time. In the final chapter, after the emperor has been brought back to life, the scene portrays a mingling of the two elements: a river gleams in the distance, and the rays of the sun shine down on the couple.

Thus this water imagery is used, as in "Hérodiade," to reflect at various stages of the work the "inner state" of various characters and situations, and in its interconnectedness it forms a web, a metaphoric structure which creates the work's meaning independently of the literal action. The use of the metaphor as a structural element implies that it possesses a degree of reality far greater than in the traditional view of the metaphor as merely a term of comparison which of course does not possess the same degree of reality as the object of comparison. Thus it is not surprising that in Die Frau ohne Schatten there are several instances where a metaphor takes on concrete form. One of these occurs in the watchmen's chorus at the end of the first act in the libretto: married couples are called a "Brücke, überm Abgrund ausgespannt / auf der die Toten wiederum ins Leben gehen," and this bridge metaphor is concretized in the final scene where the shadow of Barak's wife forms a bridge over the abyss on which the couple is joined.

Another example is the metaphor of the untying of a knot, which represents the awakening of a woman's sensuality and love, and by extension her humanity. Neither husband has been able to do this, and just as the Efrit can tell the Färberin, "der den Knoten deines Herzens lösen soll, ist dir noch nicht nahe gewesen vor dieser Stunde,"[48] so the unborn children tell the emperor that it is Barak who has untied the knot of the empress' heart.[49] If this is ultimately a metaphor for the awakening of love and higher humanity, this is a sphere which must remain closed to the diabolical nurse. Thus it is ironically appropriate that in the final chapter, when the nurse seeks to escape punishment in Keikobad's realm by fleeing on a raft, she cannot untie the knot by which the raft is fastened to the shore.

The image of chains, to which we referred earlier, though never appearing in its physical sense, does undergo a fundamental transformation. We saw earlier how Barak's wife feels bound to him with iron chains -- the most obvious meaning of bondage and entrapment. Though this is not explicitly stated here, it is clearly her feelings of guilt which "chain" her to her husband. In the final chapter, the empress meets the unborn children of the dyer couple, and is overcome by guilt:

> . . . das Gefühl der Schuld umschloß ihr Herz mit Ketten, sie fühlte sich an jene geschmiedet, in deren Dasein sie ungerufen hineingetreten war.[50]

But here her guilt is seen as the inevitable condition of humanity; confessing to one of the children, "ich hab mich vergangen," she is told, "das muß jeder sagen, der einen Fuß vor den andern setzt."[51] Guilt is thus revealed in its positive meaning of being bound up in the human community. The transformation in this image is complete in the final lines of the work, where it is disclosed:

> . . . daß auf dem Talisman an ihrer Brust längst
> die Worte des Fluchs ausgetilgt und ersetzt waren
> durch Zeichen und Verse, die das ewige Geheimnis
> der Verkettung alles Irdischen priesen.[52]

The chains which bind both the empress and the Färberin are revealed to be part of the mysterious force which draws them into humanity and the community of all earthly creatures.

And thus we have seen that the poet strikes the same balance in this work that can be observed in his essays: while the theme embodies the poet's rejection of the Symbolist cult of the sterile, lifeless, and inhuman in favor of an affirmation of human life even in its simplest, most organic aspect, the work remains deeply imbued with Symbolist aesthetics. On a thematic level, the reunions at the end between the emperor and empress and the dyer and his wife suggest the ultimate reconciliation between the ethical and the aesthetic, and thus embody Hofmannsthal's definitive rejection of the Aestheticist view that perfect beauty requires separation from life. But the metaphoric structure of the work reveals that more than a decade after the "Chandoskrise" he still makes use of what has been called the "symbolistische Technik." But once more I must reject the notion that this is simply a question of technique, for this use of metaphor implies a belief in the interpenetration of the material and spiritual realms, suggested in the Symbolist doctrine of "correspondances," and which is reflected throughout Die Frau ohne Schatten. The ability of a metaphor to be "translated" into physical reality also reflects a continuing belief in the Symbolist ideal of the magical power of language; the dual conception of language, which we discussed earlier, can be seen through the end of the poet's career, as the theme of the impotence of language, central to the 1919 comedy Der Schwierige, continues alongside the belief in the transforming and binding power of language which we have seen both in Die Frau ohne Schatten and in the essays of the last years of the poet's life.

Thus we have seen how two works of Hofmannsthal's maturity, Elektra and Die Frau ohne Schatten, demonstrate not only Hofmannsthal's thorough acquaintance with the "Scène" from Mallarmé's "Hérodiade," but also his deep preoccupation with its themes and imagery. These two of Hofmannsthal's works form a kind of hidden dialogue with "Hérodiade," running parallel in some ways and reversing elements of Mallarmé's poem in others. The relationship between the works is indeed complex. It is impossible to speak of adaptation, as one can in the relationships between Elektra, Der Bürger als Edelmann, and Der Turm with the original works by Sophocles, Molière, and Calderon. In these works Hofmannsthal is engaged in an attempt to recreate classical plays of the Western tradition in a new form, and the source of the work is never concealed; they are in a sense public tributes to these past masters of European drama. But if Elektra and Die Frau ohne Schatten are not adaptations of "Hérodiade" in this sense, Mallarmé's poem is far more than a source of motifs and imagery, such as Lenau's "Anna" and various Tales of the Arabian Nights are for Die Frau ohne Schatten. For this latter work is clearly a reply to the problems posed in "Hérodiade," and thus in borrowing elements of Mallarmé's work Hofmannsthal gives notice to all his readers familiar with the Symbolist poem that it is against this background that the problems raised in Elektra and Die Frau ohne Schatten must be viewed. This is not to suggest that one cannot understand these two works unless one is aware of their parallels to "Hérodiade"; Hofmannsthal's development of his themes in these works is certainly not so obscure that one must resort to other sources to comprehend them. Nevertheless, one cannot help but feel that the apparent helplessness of some critics, particularly in dealing with Die Frau ohne Schatten, their lack of comprehension for what seems to them the trivial theme of this work, is due to their failure to recognize as the background of the work the Aestheticist cult of the inorganic and the expression of this in Mallarmé's "Hérodiade." Taken out of context, the praise of matrimony and parenthood in Die Frau ohne Schatten seems conventional and unnecessary; seen in its proper context, however, it is a uniquely life-affirming and humanistic statement.

And thus the dilemma posed by Symbolism -- the tension between the actual poetic practice and theory of Symbolism, which was such a liberating influence for Hofmannsthal and other German poets of his generation, and the negative conscquences of the life-denying Aestheticist world view -- is finally resolved by the poet in this work. Where the Aestheticist (or, for that matter, the Puritan moralist) would see an irreconcilable conflict between the aesthetic and the ethical, Hofmannsthal shows that these two realms are not only reconcilable, but that only through their reconciliation can either life or beauty be achieved and sustained.

NOTES

[1] Mario Praz, The Romantic Agony, trans. Angus Davidson, 2nd edition (London and New York: Oxford University Press, 1970), p. 31.

[2] Stéphane Mallarmé, Les noces d'Hérodiade. Mystère, ed. Garner Davies (Paris: Gallimard, 1959).

[3] Letter to Henri Cazalis of April 1866 in Correspondance 1862-1871, ed. Henri Mondor and Jean-Pierre Richard (Paris: Gallimard, 1959), p. 207.

[4] Correspondance 1862-1871, p. 193

[5] Robert de Montesquiou, Diptyque de Flandre, Triptyque de France (Paris: Chiberre, 1921), p. 235.

[6] Peter Szondi, Das lyrische Drama des Fin-de-siècle (Frankfurt: Suhrkamp, 1975), p. 95.

[7] Szondi, pp. 98-99. It hardly seems necessary to assume, as does R. G. Cohn in Toward the Poems of Mallarmé (Berkeley and Los Angeles: University of California Press, 1965), pp. 80-81, that Hérodiade here confesses that everything she has said has been a lie; we have seen how her self-delusions and dreams of escape alternate with an increasing degree of self-knowledge.

[8] Correspondance 1862-1871, p. 141.

[9] Charles Mauron, Introduction to the Psychoanalysis of Mallarmé, trans. Archibald Henderson, Jr., and Will L. McLendon (Berkeley and Los Angeles: University of California Press, 1963).

[10] Trans. David Greene in The Complete Greek Tragedies IV, ed. David Greene and Richmond Lattimore (New York: Modern Library, 1957), p. 145.

[11] Complete Greek Tragedies IV, p. 145.

[12] DII, p. 10.

[13] DII, pp. 10-11.

[14] DII, p. 13.

[15] DII, p. 19.

[16] DII, p. 20.

[17] DII, pp. 20-21.

[18] DII, p. 40.

[19] DII, pp. 62-63.

[20] A, p. 131.

[21] A, p. 181.

[22] The two versions are compared in depth in Belma Çakmur, Hofmannsthals Erzählung "Die Frau ohne Schatten" (Ankara: Türk Tarih Kurumu Basimevi, 1952), to which I refer the reader.

[23] DIII, p. 479.

[24] See the very illuminating study by Károly Csúri, "Hugo von Hofmannsthals späte Erzählung: Die Frau ohne Schatten. Struktur und Strukturvergleich" in Studia Poetica, 2 (1980), pp. 125-257.

[25] F. C. St. Aubyn, "Hérodiade: eine Frau mit Schatten?", Revue de littérature comparée, 33, No. 1 (1959), 40-49.

[26] See Handwörterbuch des deutschen Aberglaubens, 9, ed. E. Hoffmann-Krayer and Hanns Bächtold-Stäubli (Berlin: Walter de Gruyter & Co., 1941), pp. 132ff.

[27] Mallarmé was also familiar with this work, and disliked it. (Correspondance 1862-1871, p. 156).

[28] The Types of the Folktale: A Classification and Bibliography, 2nd revision (Helsinki: Suomalainen Tiedeakatemia, 1964), p. 259.

[29] E, p. 255.

[30] E, pp. 267-68.

[31] E, p. 330.

[32] E, p. 255.

[33] DIII, p. 223.

[34] E, p. 328.

[35] E, p. 257.

[36] E, p. 271.

[37] E, pp. 290-91.

[38] E, p. 286.

[39] E, pp. 273-74.

[40] E, p. 286.

[41] E, p. 282.

[42] E, p. 285.

[43] E, p. 330.

[44] E, p. 347.
[45] E, p. 256.
[46] E, p. 340.
[47] E, p. 265.
[48] E, p. 288.
[49] E, p. 319.
[50] E, p. 364.
[51] E, p. 361.
[52] E, p. 375.

CONCLUSION

If it is the fate of many great writers to be misunderstood during their own lives and for some time beyond, it is fair to say that few major writers of modern times have had worse fortune in this regard than Hofmannsthal. For a few brief years in the 1890s and the beginning of this century, he enjoyed a considerable reputation as the Wunderkind of German literature, the youthful creator of lyrics of a perfection rarely seen since Goethe. But it was ironically this reputation which contributed to the widespread incomprehension of and even hostility to the new directions his work took following the turn of the century. The comment of Hermann Bahr that if Hofmannsthal had only died at the age of twenty-five he would have been remembered as the most beautiful figure in literary history, was just a particularly malicious formulation of a widespread attitude. But if the poet's turn to popular forms earned him the enmity of contemporary artistic circles, the subtlety of his art and even his own temperament barred him from ever becoming a popular writer. Thus just as the adherents of Aestheticism were branding him a traitor to the cause, the general reading public continued to view him as an aesthete and even a decadent. It was this latter reputation, added to the fact that his paternal grandfather was

Jewish, which led to the banning of his works by the Nazis, thus putting an end to the study and performance of his works in Germany and (after 1938) his native Austria until 1945.

The renewed critical interest in Hofmannsthal since the war, though welcome, cannot be regarded as wholly a vindication of the poet. Though critics have taken many different paths, the main thrust of post-war Hofmannsthal criticism, following the lead of Richard Alewyn, has been the attempt to destroy the prevailing view of Hofmannsthal as an aesthete or decadent. This effort was of course entirely proper and overdue. But the efforts of many critics go further than this, and this is where the problem arises. Following the experience of Nazism, there was and is a belief that Aestheticism, by turning its back on social and political realities, helped prepare the way for Fascism, where it did not actually advance the cause under the guise of artistic indifference to politics. This belief has for understandable reasons been particularly strong in the German-speaking lands. Though the immediate effect of this was a rejection of explicitly Aestheticist and anti-social art, it has led more generally to a regrettable tendency to judge artists largely by their social and political attitudes. In response to this, critics seized on Hofmannsthal's very real attempts to find a <u>Weg zum Sozialen</u> in his work, and tried to present Hofmannsthal to a new generation as a socially engaged artist. This is an effort doomed to failure, and one which can only lead to a new distortion of the poet's work. It is this, I believe, that accounts for the reluctance of modern Hofmannsthal scholars such as Böschenstein and Exner to acknowledge the poet's indebtedness to the "aestheticist" movement of French Symbolism. The problem is that in a contemporary German context, social engagement generally implies a Marxist or at least a progressive commitment to fundamental social and economic reforms. But a young German who turns to Hofmannsthal's writings will soon discover that the poet's political instincts were deeply conservative and aristocratic, that his thinking on social issues was more akin to the nineteenth-century British tradition of Coleridge, Carlyle, and Ruskin than to Marxism or even Liberalism, and that his specific political commitments and actions betrayed a naiveté which is somewhat embarrassing to his admirers today. A generation whose philosophy (or at least whose rhetoric) is Marxist and whose literary idol is Bertolt Brecht will inevitably tend to dismiss Hofmannsthal as a reactionary, irrelevant in his concerns and "old-fashioned" in his manner. And so it is that, apart from the obligatory "Jedermann" at Salzburg and the three or four Strauss operas which are regularly performed, none of Hofmannsthal's stage works have found a firm place in the standard repertory; even the centennial of the poet's birth several years ago has done little to alter this fact.

The extent to which Hofmannsthal's reputation has been essentially a victim of circumstances can best be illustrated through a comparison with the reputation of T. S. Eliot, a writer whose work is parallel to Hofmannsthal's in several respects. Both were crucially influenced by French Symbolist poetry. Both were among those poets responsible for the revival of verse drama as a legitimte modern form. Above all, both were deeply conscious of being inheritors of a centuries-old European literary tradition, and reflected this consciousness in their work as prolific essayists; the views which Eliot pronounced in the famous essay "Tradition and the Individual Talent" are ones which Hofmannsthal almost certainly would have accepted without reservation. And yet, in spite of the fact that Eliot's poetic oeuvre, generally speaking, presents more formidable obstacles to the general reader, both formally and intellectually, than does Hofmannsthal's, Eliot's literary reputation in the English-speaking world is so firmly established that it is hard to conceive of his being dislodged from the literary pantheon. Because of the different history of the English-speaking lands in the past century, there has not been such a tendency to judge artists according to their political beliefs, and thus several generations of educated Americans and Britons, even if their own political views were somewhat to the left of the national center, nevertheless were not distracted by Eliot's political, social, and religious conservatism from an appreciation of his work; even the outspoken Fascism of Ezra Pound has by and large not prevented an appreciation of his contributions to twentieth-century poetry. Ignoring this fact, some would explain Hofmannsthal's relative "failure" by suggesting that he was not a writer of the same caliber, but this view scarcely seems tenable. Hofmannsthal is arguably the finest writer of comedies in the German language; his lyric production, though small in quantity, has earned him a place among the greatest German lyric poets which few would deny; and there is an increasing critical recognition today that he belongs in the ranks of the greatest prose stylists of the German language. Of what other German writer since Goethe can it be said that he produced works of the first rank in the diverse fields of lyric poetry, comedy, tragedy, narrative and discursive prose?

* * *

In the light of this rather grim view of the state of general appreciation of Hofmannsthal's accomplishments, it may well be asked what this study of Hofmannsthal's relation to one particular literary movement can hope to achieve. This question can best be answered by referring to the generally recognized fact that nineteenth-century Symbolism was one of the main sources of literary Modernism in prose as well as poetry.[1] Thus the failure to recognize Hofmannsthal's adoption of Symbolist aesthetics and poetic technique is largely responsible for the widespread notion that Hofmannsthal is essentially a nineteenth-century artist, a view advanced by Hugo Friedrich in his otherwise admirable study Die Struktur der modernen Lyrik.² This impression is fostered by the fact that Hofmannsthal's work lacks the "shocking" qualities of the most radical Modernism. But this study has suggested that Hofmannsthal's work represents a radical departure from the tradition of nineteenth-century German poetry, and thus one goal of this work has been to establish Hofmannsthal as a writer of our time, one whose work must not be relegated to a distant past.

It is precisely when one regards Hofmannsthal in the context of Modernism that his full importance and stature becomes clear. Few would deny today the quality of the major works by those artists in the first two or three decades of this century who are generally included under the banner of Modernism. And yet even among the most fervent admirers of this art, there are few today who are not disturbed by certain aspects of it, aspects which are most clearly defined by José Ortega y Gasset in his classic 1925 essay "The Dehumanization of Art."

Ortega y Gasset lists Mallarmé among the key father-figures of the new art, and specifically mentions the "realization" of the metaphor as an example of the inversion of normal perspective which characterizes the new art. Thus Hofmannsthal would seem to belong among the artists referred to here. But let us examine some of the tendencies which Ortega y Gasset sees in the new art. The first two he cites are the tendency to dehumanize art and the tendency to avoid living forms.³ These are both characteristic of Symbolism, as we have seen, and it is precisely these aspects of the movement which Hofmannsthal rejects. Ortega y Gasset describes, with obvious disdain, the traditional, "human" response to a work of art:

> A man likes a play when has has become interested in the human destinies presented to him, when the love and hatred, the joys and sorrows of the personages so move his heart that he participates in it all as though it were happening in real life. 4

For him there is a fundamental opposition between this "human" response and a response which looks for the specifically aesthetic qualities of the work of art and which is concerned mainly with form. This is an opposition which Hofmannsthal rejects; what makes him almost unique among the writers of Modernism is that in a work such as <u>Die Frau ohne Schatten</u> he is able to satisfy these desires of the ordinary public while at the same time constructing a literary work of a degree of formal complexity to satisfy the most exacting aesthetic taste. A further tendency cited by Ortega y Gasset is "to see to it that the work of art is nothing but a work of art," or to put it another way, to maintain a clear distinction between life and art. We saw in the second chapter that Hofmannsthal did insist on a fundamental separation between art and life, but this does not imply for him, as it does for Ortega y Gasset, that one must turn one's back on the general public; for Hofmannsthal any art which does not contain life and which does not reach out to a living audience is fundamentally dead. Ortega y Gasset also lists an essentially negative attitude towards literary tradition as a tendency of the new art; clearly this is not the case with Hofmannsthal, but it is no more true of the Modernism of Eliot or Pound.

It is with this background in mind that it becomes possible to define Hofmannsthal's position in modern literary history, and to defend his claim to be ranked among the great writers of the twentieth century. As were most of the writers of Modernism, Hofmannsthal was acutely aware of the exhaustion of nineteenth-century literary forms, and at every stage of his career he created works whose form and style represented a significant break from the work of his contemporaries and his immediate predecessors. The fact that so often he looked back to the great works of the Western tradition as models does not separate him, as we have seen, from the Modernism of Eliot and Pound. And yet where so many Modernist writers accepted the fractured nature of modern life and the fundamental gap separating modern art and artists from a larger audience, Hofmannsthal throughout his career emphasized the binding power of art, its ability and its duty to create the myths which unite the human community from class to class, from nation to nation, and from generation to generation.

NOTES

[1] See, for example, Edmund Wilson, Axël's Castle (New York: Scribner & Sons, 1931) and Hugo Friedrich, Die Struktur der modernen Lyrik, new expanded edition (Hamburg: Rowohlt, 1956).

[2] Friedrich, pp. 10, 18.

[3] José Ortega y Gasset, The Dehumanizaion of Art, trans. Helen Wyl (Princeton: Princeton University Press, 1968), p. 14.

[4] Ortega y Gasset, p. 8.

BIBLIOGRAPHY

I. Primary Sources

Baudelaire, Charles Pierre. <u>Oeuvres Complètes</u>. Ed. Y.-G. Le Dantec and Claude Pichois. Rev. ed. Paris: Gallimard, 1959.

Hofmannsthal, Hugo von. <u>Gesammelte Werke in Einzelausgaben</u>. Ed. Herbert Steiner. Stockholm and Frankfurt: Fischer Verlag, 1946 onward.

Individual volumes:

<u>Die Erzählungen</u>. 1945, 3rd ed. 1953.

<u>Gedichte und lyrische Dramen</u>. 1946, 2nd ed. 1952, rpt. 1970.

<u>Lustpiele I</u>. 1947, rpt. 1959.

<u>Lustpiele II</u>. 1948, rpt. 1965.

<u>Lustpiele III</u>. 1956, rpt. 1968.

<u>Lustpiele IV</u>. 1956, rpt. 1973.

<u>Prosa I</u>. 1950, rpt. 1956.

<u>Prosa II</u>. 1951, rpt. 1959.

<u>Prosa III</u>. 1953, rpt. 1964.

<u>Prosa IV</u>. 1955, rpt. 1966.

<u>Dramen I</u>. 1953, rpt. 1964.

<u>Dramen II</u>. 1954, rpt. 1966.

<u>Dramen III</u>. 1957, rpt. 1969.

<u>Dramen IV</u>. 1958, rpt. 1970.

Aufzeichnungen. 1959, rpt. 1973.

Mallarmé, Stéphane. Les noces d'Hérodiade: Mystère. Ed. Gardner Davies. Paris: Gallimard, 1959.

Mallarmé, Stéphane. Oeuvres Complètes. Ed. Henri Mondor and Jean-Pierre Richard. Paris: Gallimard, 1970.

Verlaine, Paul Marie. Oeuvres poétiques complètes. Ed. Jacques Borel and Y.-G. Le Dantec. Rev. ed. Paris: Gallimard, 1973.

II. Correspondence

Briefwechsel zwischen George und Hofmannsthal. Ed. Robert Boehringer. 2nd ed. Munich and Düsseldorf: Helmut Küpper, 1953.

Hofmannsthal, Hugo von. Briefe 1890-1901. Berlin: S. Fischer, 1935.

Mallarmé, Stéphane. Correspondance 1862-1871. Ed. Henri Mondor and Jean-Pierre Richard. Paris: Gallimard, 1959.

III. Secondary Sources

A. Works on Hofmannsthal

Alewyn, Richard. Über Hugo von Hofmannsthal. 3rd ed. Göttingen: Vandenhoeck & Ruprecht, 1963.

Aspetsberger, Friedrich. "Hofmannsthal und D'Annunzio." Hofmannsthal-Forschungen I. Basel: Hugo von Hofmannsthal-Gesellschaft, 1971.

Block, Haskell. "Hofmannsthal and the Symbolist Drama." Transactions of the Wisconsin Academy of Sciences, Arts, and Letters, 48 (1959), 161-178.

Bolliger, Bruno. "Die Zerstörung des Mythos vom Ästheten Hofmannsthal." Schweizer Monatshefte, 53, No. 10 (1974), 724-730.

Bollnow, Otto Friedrich. "Der Lebensbegriff des jungen Hugo von Hofmannsthal." Unruhe und Geborgenheit im Weltbild neuerer Dichter. Stuttgart: Kohlhammer, 1953, pp. 15-30.

Böschenstein, Bernhard. "Hofmannsthal und der europäische Symbolismus." Hofmannsthal-Forschungen II. Freiburg: Hugo von Hofmannsthal-Gesellschaft, 1974, pp. 73-87.

Brecht, Walther. "Hugo von Hofmannsthals 'Ad me ipsum' und seine Bedeutung." Jahrbuch des freien deutschen Hochstifts 1930. Ansbach: E. Brügel & Sohn, 1930, pp. 319-53.

Brinkmann, Richard. "Hofmannsthal und die Sprache." Deutsche Vierteljahrsschrift, 35, No. 1 (1961), 69-95.

Broch, Hermann. "Hofmannsthal und seine Zeit: Eine Studie." Dichten und Erkennen: Essays Band I. Ed. and introd. by Hannah Arendt. Zürich: Rhein-Verlag, 1955, pp. 43-181.

Çakmur, Belma. Hofmannsthals Erzählung "Die Frau ohne Schatten": Studien zu Werk und Innenwelt des Dichters. Ankara: Türk Tarih Kurumu Basimevi, 1952.

Csúri, Károly. "Hugo von Hofmannsthals späte Erzählung: Die Frau ohne Schatten. Struktur und Vergleich." Studia Poetica, 2 (1980), 125-257.

Dormer, Lore Muerdel. "Die Truggestalt der Kaiserin und Oscar Wilde: Zur Metaphorik in Hofmannsthals Drama 'Der Kaiser und die Hexe.'" Zeitschrift für deutsche Philologie, 96 (1977), 579-86.

Exner, Richard. Hugo von Hofmannsthals "Lebenslied": Eine Studie. Heidelberg: Carl Winter, 1964.

Faucard, Geneviève. "Une expérience privilégiée du moi et sa fonction dans le lyrisme de Hofmannsthal." Etudes Germaniques, 27, No. 3 (1972), 388-406.

Foldenauer, Karl. "Hugo von Hofmannsthal und die französische Literatur des 19. und 20. Jahrhunderts." Diss. Tübingen 1958.

Goff, Penrith. "Hugo von Hofmannsthal and Walter Pater." Comparative Literature Studies, 7, No. 1 (1970), 1-11.

Graf, Erich. "Die Frau ohne Schatten: Eine Sinndeutung der Handlung." Richard Strauss-Blätter, 7 (1976), 19-29.

Gray, Mary O. P. "Hugo von Hofmannsthal and Nineteenth-Century French Symbolism." Diss. Dublin 1951.

Hammelman, Hanns. Hugo von Hofmannsthal. Studies in European Literature and Thought. London: Bowes & Bowes, 1957.

Hugo von Hofmannsthal: Die Gestalt des Dichters im Spiegel seiner Freunde. Ed. Helmut Fiechtner. Vienna: Humboldt Verlag, 1949.

Jaszi, Andrew O. "Die Idee des Lebens in Hofmannsthals Jugendwerk 1890-1900." Germanic Review, 24, No. 2 (1961), 69-95.

Jenkinson, D. E. "The Poetry of Transition: Some Aspects of the Interpretation of Hofmannsthal's Lyrics." German Life and Letters, 27 (1973-74), 294-303.

Kenkel, Konrad. "Die Funktion der Sprache bei Hofmannsthal vor und nach der Chandos-Krise." Texte und Kontexte. Ed. Manfred Durzak, Eberhard Reichmann, and Ulrich Weisstein. Bern and Munich: Francke-Verlag, 1973, pp. 89-102.

Knaus, Jakob. Hofmannsthals Weg zur Oper "Die Frau ohne Schatten." Berlin and New York: Walter de Gruyter, 1971.

Kobel, Erwin. Hugo von Hofmannsthal. Berlin: de Gruyter, 1971.

Koch, Hans-Albrecht. "'Fastkontrapunktlich streng.'" Jahrburch des freien deutschen Hochstifts 1971. Tubingen: Max Niemeyer Verlag, 1971, pp. 456-478.

Mayer, Hans. "Die Frau ohne Schatten." Jahresring, 25 (1978-79), 221-40.

Metzeler, Werner. Ursprung und Krise von Hofmannsthals Mystik. Munich: Bergstadt Verlag, 1956.

Naef, Karl J. Hugo von Hofmannsthals Wesen und Werk. Zürich and Leipzig: Max Niehans, 1938.

Pantle, Sherill Hahn. "Die Frau ohne Schatten" by Hugo von Hofmannsthal and Richard Strauss. An Analysis of Text, Music and their Relationship. Berne/Frankfurt/Las Vegas: Herbert Lang, 1978.

Pestalozzi, Karl. Sprachskepsis und Sprachmagie im Werk des jungen Hofmannsthals. Zürich: Atlantis Verlag, 1958.

Reid, J. H. "'Draußen sind wir zu finden . . .': The Development of a Hofmannsthal Symbol." German Life and Letters, 27 (1973-74), 35-51.

Rey, William H. "Die Drohung der Zeit in Hofmannsthals Frühwerk." Euphorion, 48, No. 3 (1954), 280-310.

Ritter, Ellen. "Über den Begriff Praeexistenz bei Hugo von Hofmannsthal." Germanisch-Romanische Monatsschrift, 22, No. 2 (1972), 197-200.

Ryan, Judith. "Die 'allomatische Lösung': Gespaltene Persönlichkeit und Konfiguration bei Hugo von Hofmannsthal." Deutsche Vierteljahrsschrift, 44, No. 2 (1970), 189-207.

Saas, Christa. "Das Sonettproblem bei Hofmannsthal." Paper delivered at the Hofmannsthal Seminar of the 1976 MLA Convention in New York City.

Schaber, Steven C. "The Lord Chandos Letter in the Light of Hofmannsthal's Lyric Decade." Germanic Review, 45, No. 1 (1970), 52-58.

----------. "Novalis' 'Monolog' and Hofmannsthal's 'Ein Brief': Two Poets in Search of a Language." German Quarterly, 47, No. 2 (1974), 204-214.

Sondrup, Steven P. "The Contexts and Concepts of 'Leben' in the Poetry of Hugo von Hofmannsthal." Colloquia Germanica, 11 (1978), 289-297.

----------. Hofmannsthal and the French Symbolist Tradition. Berne/Frankfurt: Herbert Lang, 1976.

----------. "Three Notes on Symbolism by Hugo von Hofmannsthal." Modern Austrian Literature, 9, No. 2 (1976), 1-9.

Steffens, Hans. "Hofmannsthals Übernahme der symbolistischen Technik." Literatur und Geistesgeschichte. Ed. Reinhold Grimm and Conrad Wiedemann. Berlin: Erich Schmidt Verlag, 1968, pp. 271-79.

Tarot, Rolf. Hugo von Hofmannsthal: Daseinsformen und dichterische Struktur. Tübingen: M. Niemeyer, 1970.

Vanhelleputte, Michel. "Hofmannsthal und Maeterlinck." Hofmannsthal-Forschungen I. Basel: Hugo von Hofmannsthal-Gesellschaft, 1971, pp. 85-98.

Weber, Eugene M. "A Chronology of Hofmannsthal's Poems." Euphorion, 63 (1969), 284-328.

----------. "Hofmannsthal und Oscar Wilde." Hofmannsthal-Forschungen I. Basel: Hugo von Hofmannsthal-Gesellschaft, 1971, pp. 99-106.

Wunberg, Gotthart. Der frühe Hofmannsthal: Schizophrenie als dichterische Struktur. Stuttgart: W. Kohlhammer Verlag, 1965.

Wyss, Hugo. Die Frau in der Dichtung Hofmannsthals. Zürich: Max Niehans Verlag, 1954.

B. Works on Mallarmé and French Symbolism

Block, Haskell M. Mallarmé and the Symbolist Drama. Detroit: Wayne State University Press, 1963.

Cohn, Robert Greer. *Toward the Poems of Mallarmé*. Berkeley: University of California Press, 1965.

Cornell, Kenneth. *The Symbolist Movement*. New Haven: Yale University Press, 1951.

Davies, Gardner, introd. *Les noces d'Hérodiade: Mystère*. By Stéphane Mallarmé. Paris: Gallimard, 1959.

Fowlie, Wallace. *Mallarmé*. Chicago: University of Chicago Press, 1962.

Lehmann, Andrew George. *The Symbolist Aesthetic in France, 1885-1895*. 2nd ed. Oxford: Blackwell, 1968.

Mauron, Charles. *Introduction to the Psychoanalysis of Mallarmé*. Trans. Archibald Henderson, Jr. and Will L. McLendon. Berkeley and Los Angeles: University of California Press, 1963.

Michaud, Guy. *Mallarmé*. Trans. Marie Collins and Bertha Humez. New York: New York University Press, 1965.

----------. *Message poétique du symbolisme*. 3 vols. Paris: Nizet, 1961.

Montesquiou, Robert de. *Diptyque de Flandre, Triptyque de France*. Paris: Chiberre, 1921.

Noulet, Emilie. *L'oeuvre poétique de Stéphane Mallarmé*. Paris: E. Droz, 1940; rpt. Bruxelles: Antoine, 1974.

Poulet, Georges. "Mallarmé." *The Interior Distance*. Trans. Elliot Coleman. Baltimore: Johns Hopkins Press, 1959, pp. 235-83.

Raymond, Marcel. De Baudelaire a Surréalisme. Rev. ed.
Paris: José Corti, 1963.

Richard, Jean-Pierre. L'univers imaginaire de Mallarmé.
Paris: Eidtions du Seuil, 1961.

Richardson, Joanna. Verlaine. New York: Viking, 1971.

Schmidt, Albert Marie. La littérature symboliste (1870-1900).
Paris: Presses Universitaires de France, 1960.

Starkie, Enid. Baudelaire. New York: G. P. Putnam's Sons, 1933; rpt. London: Faber & Faber, 1957.

Symons, Arthur. The Symbolist Movement in Literature. Rev. ed. New York: Dutton, 1958.

Thibaudet, Albert. La poésie de Stéphane Mallarmé. Paris: Gallimard, 1926.

Wais, Kurt. Mallarmé. 2nd ed. Munich: C. H. Beck, 1952.

C. Comparative General, and Other Works

Arne, Antti and Stith Thompson. The Types of the Folktale: A Classification and Bibliography. 2nd rev. Helsinki: Suomalainen Tiedeakatemia, 1964.

Bahr, Hermann. Studien zur Kritik der Moderne. Frankfurt: Rütten & Loening, 1894.

----------. Zur Kritik der Moderne: Erste Reihe. Zürich: J. Schabelitz, 1890.

Beardsley, Monroe C. and W. K. Wimsatt. "The Intentional Fallacy." W. K. Wimsatt, The Verbal Icon. Lexington: University of Kentucky Press, 1967, pp. 3-18.

Blätter für die Kunst, 1892-1919. 6 vol. reprint. Berlin: Helmut Küpper, 1968.

Boehringer, Robert. Mein Bild von Stefan George. 2nd ed. Düsseldorf & Munich: Helmut Küpper, 1967.

Böschenstein, Bernhard. "Wirkungen des französischen Symbolismus auf die deutsche Lyrik der Jahrhundertwende." Euphorion 58, No. 4 (1964), 375-95.

Bowra, Cecil Maurice. The Heritage of Symbolism. London: Macmillan & Co. Ltd., 1947.

Duthie, Enid Lowrie. L'influence du Symbolisme français dans le renouveau poétique de l'Allemagne. Paris: Honoré Champion, 1933.

Eliot, Thomas Stearnes. To Criticize the Critic. New York: Farrar, Straus & Giroux, 1965.

Friedrich, Hugo. Die Struktur der modernen Lyrik. New expanded edition. Hamburg: Rowohlt, 1956.

Gaunt, William. The Aesthetic Adventure. New York: Harcourt, Brace & Co., 1945.

Gibbs, Beverly Jean. "Impressionism as a Literary Movement." Modern Language Journal, 36, No. 4 (1952), 175-83.

Hamann, Richard and Jost Hermand. Impresisonismus. New Ed. Berlin: Akademie Verlag, 1960.

Hough, Graham Goulden. The Last Romantics. New York: Barnes & Noble, 1961.

Jackson, Holbrook. Dreamers of Dreams: The Rise and Fall of

Nineteenth-Century Idealism. New York: Farrar, Straus, 1949.

----------. The Eighteen-Nineties: A Review of Art and Ideas at the Close of the Nineteenth Century. New ed. with introd. Karl Beckson. New York: Capricorn Books, 1966.

Janik, Allan and Stephen Toulmin. Wittgenstein's Vienna. New York: Simon & Schuster, 1973.

Jost, Dominik. Literarischer Jugendstil. Stuttgart: J. B. Metzler, 1960.

Kluckhohn, Paul. "Die Wende vom 19. zum 20. Jahrhundert in der deutschen Dichtung." Deutsche Vierteljahrsschrift, 29, No. 1 (1955), 1-19.

Mravlag, Lene. "Der Symbolismus in Frankreich, der Symbolismus in Deutschland, und Versuch einer Gegenüberstellung." Diss. Vienna 1938.

Ortega y Gasset, José. The Dehumanization of Art and Other Essays on Art, Culture, and Literature. Trans. Helen Wyl. New ed. Princeton: Princeton University Press, 1968.

Perl, Walter A. "Österreichischer Symbolismus und Jugendstil." Modern Austrian Literature, 5, No. 3 (1972), 70-82.

Petersen, Julius. Die Sehnsucht nach dem dritten Reich in deutscher Sage und Dichtung. Stuttgart: J. B. Metzler, 1934.

Pollak, Ilse. "Die Einwirkung der französischen Paranassiens und Symbolisten auf Stefan George und seinen Kreis." Diss.

Vienna, 1932.

Praz, Mario. The Romantic Agony. Trans. Angus Davidson. 2nd ed. London and New York: Oxford University Press, 1970.

St. Aubyn, F. C. "Hérodiade: Eine Frau mit Schatten?" Revue de littérature comparée, 33, No. 1 (1949), 40-49.

"Schatten." Handwörterbuch des deutschen Aberglaubens, 9, 132ff. Ed. E. Hoffmann-Krayer and Hanns Bächtold-Stäubli. Berlin: Walter de Gruyter, 1941.

Sophocles. Electra. Trans. David Green. The Complete Greek Tragedies. Vol. IV. Ed. David Greene and Richmond Lattimore. New York: The Modern Library, 1957.

Stahl, E. L. "The Genesis of Symbolist Theories in Germany." Modern Language Review, 41 (1946), 306ff.

Staiger, Emil. Grundbegriffe der Poetik. Zürich: Atlantis Verlag, 1946.

Starkie, Enid. From Gautier to Eliot: The Influence of France on English Literature, 1851-1939. London: Hutchinson, 1960.

Steiner, Herbert. "A Note on Symbolism." Yale French Studies, No. 9 (1952), 36-39.

Szondi, Peter. Das lyrische Drama des Fin-de-siècle. Ed. Henriette Beese. Frankfurt: Suhrkamp, 1975.

Temple, Ruth Z. The Critic's Alchemy: A Study of the Introduction of French Symbolism into England. New York; Twayne, 1953.

Thibaudet, Albert. French Literature from 1795 to Our Era.

Trans. Charles Lam Markmann. New York: Funk & Wagnalls, 1967.

Thomèse, Ika Alida. Romantik und Neuromantik mit besonderer Berücksichtigung Hugo von Hofmannsthals. The Hague: Martinus Nijhoff, 1923.

Vordtriede, Werner. Novalis und die französischen Symbolisten: Zur Entstehungsgeschichte des dichterischen Symbols. Stuttgart: Kohlhammer, 1963.

Weisstein, Ulrich. "Impressionism." Encyclopedia of Poetry and Poetics. Ed. Alex Preminger. Princeton: Princeton University Press, 1965, 381ff.

Williams, Raymond. Culture and Society, 1780-1950. New York: Harper & Row, 1958.

Willoughby, L. A. "Oscar Wilde and Goethe: The Life of Art and the Art of Life." Publications of the English Goethe Society, NS 35 (1965), 1-37.

Wilson, Edmund. Axël's Castle. New York: Scribner & Sons, 1931.

Ziolkowski, Theodore. "Gerhart Hauptmann and the Problem of Language." Germanic Review, 38, No. 4 (1963), 295-306.

----------. "James Joyces Epiphanie und die Überwindung der Wirklichkeit in der modernen deutschen Prosa." Deutsche Vierteljahrsschrift, 35, No. 4 (1961), 594-616.

----------. "Natur als Nachahmung der Kunst bei Goethe." Wissen aus Erfahrungen: Werkbegriff und Interpretation heute. Ed. Alexander von Bormann. Tübingen: Max

Niemeyer Verlag, 1976, pp. 242-255.

----------. *The Novels of Hermann Hesse: A Study in Theme and Structure*. Princeton: Princeton University Press, 1965.

INDEX

All names mentioned in the text (excluding notes and bibliography) are included, as well as all works by Hofmannsthal. Works by other authors are listed only if they are discussed in some detail.

Aeschylus, 194-95

Alewyn, Richard, 105-06, 236

Amiel, Henri-Frédéric, 10-11, 117

Andrian, Leopold, 17, 62, 64

Arne, Antti, 211

Aubanel, Theodore, 190

Bahr, Hermann, 4-12, 15, 71, 235

Banville, Théodore de, 8, 76

Barrès, Maurice, 10, 11, 75

Baudelaire, Charles, 2-3, 5-7, 9, 12-14, 16, 28-36, 43-44, 46-47, 59, 62, 72-73, 88, 99-101, 118, 137, 148-49, 155, 159, 161, 175, 183, 189

    "La vie antérieure," 28-35, 46

Beardsley, Monroe C., 56-58

Block, Haskell, 76-77

Böcklin, Arnold, 1

Böschenstein, Bernhard, 237

Bourget, Paul, 10

Brecht, Bertolt, 237

Brecht, Walther, 14, 25, 54, 64, 88

Brentano, Clemens, 58, 147

Broch, Hermann, 80

Burne-Jones, Edward, 123
Byron, George Gordon, Lord, 169, 192
Carlyle, Thomas, 237
Chamisso, Adelbert von, 210
Claudel, Paul, 75, 204
Coleridge, Samuel Taylor, 58, 237
Coppée, Francois, 103, 142
Corneille, Pierre, 59
D'Annunzio, Gabriele, 14, 116, 126-34, 170
Dante, 124
Davies, Gardner, 171-72
Droste-Hülshoff, Annette von, 58
Dubray, Gabriel, 5
Eichendorff, Joseph von, 58
Eliot, Thomas Stearns, 238, 242
Exner, Richard, 237
Freud, Sigmund, 10
Friedrich, Hugo, 239
Gautier, Théophile, 7, 100
Geibel, Emanuel, 61
George, Stefan, 4, 12-16, 18, 46, 54, 62-63, 68, 77, 80, 87, 118, 134-136, 148, 157-58, 173, 204
Ghil, René, 3
Gibbs, Beverly Jean, 72
Goethe, Johann Wolfgang von, 55, 57-58, 61, 102, 105, 116, 128, 170, 188, 192, 203, 235, 239

Hauptmann, Gerhart, 48

Hearn, Lafcadio, 26-27

Hebbel, Friedrich, 58, 147

Hölderlin, Friedrich 46, 61

Hofmannsthal, Hugo von, passim
  Prose works: Ad me ipsum, 25-28, 37, 40-41, 45, 85, 115, 118, 134; "Algernon Charles Swinburne," 116, 118-24, 126, 128-29; "Ankündigung" for the Neue deutsche Beiträge, 156; "Bahrs Roman Die Mutter," 5-6, 116-17; "Bildlicher Ausdruck," 73; "Ein Brief" (Chandos letter), 4, 47, 103-105, 116, 142-45, 161; Das Buch der Freunde, 125; "Die Bühne als Traumbild," 146-47; "Der Dichter und diese Zeit," 70, 152-55, 204; "Einige Worte als Vorrede zu St.-J. Perse, 'Anabasis,'" 158-60; "Eleonora Duse II," 1; "Francis Vielé-Griffins Gedichte," 16-17, 64, 134-35, 160; "Gabriele D'Annunzio I," 126-29; "Gabriele D'Annunzio II," 126, 129-31; "Gedichte von Stefan George," 134-36, 141, 148; "Das Gespräch über Gedichte," 4, 88, 147-52; "Lafcadio Hearn," 26; "Lucidor," 204; "Maurice Barrès," 10-11, 75; "Eine Monographie," 53, 55; "Der neue Roman von D'Annunzio," 126, 131-34; "Poesie und Leben," 136-40, 141, 148, 152; "Schöne Sprache," 155-56; "Das Schrifttum als geistiger Raum der Nation," 157-58; "Sebastian Melmoth," 152; "Südfranzösische Eindrücke," 1; "Das Tagebuch eines Willenskranken," 10-11, 117; "Theodore de Banville," 8; "Über moderne englische Malerei," 124-26.

  Poems: "Ballade des äußeren Lebens," 63-66; "Die Beiden," 39; "Blühende Bäume," 67; "Dein Antlitz," 63, 79-80; "Erlebnis," 81-83; "Frage," 79, 83; "Für mich," 51; "Gedankenspuk," 85; "Hirtenknabe singt," 83; "Idylle," 84-86, 191, 206-07; "Der Kaiser von China spricht," 83-84; "Ein Knabe," 36-39, 41-42, 44; "Lebenslied," 42, 121; "Regen in der Dämmerung," 63; "Sturmnacht," 67; "Terzinen: Über Vergänglichkeit," 35, 63; "Verse zum Gedächtnis des Schauspielers Joseph Kainz," 145; "Vor Tag," 145; "Vorfrühling," 63, 68-71; "Was ist die Welt," 66-67; "Weltgeheimnis," 39-40, 52-53; "Wolken," 67-71.

  Theater: Alkestis, 192, 203; Ariadne auf Naxos, 196; Das Bergwerk zu Falun, 191; Der Bürger als Edelmann, 228; Cristinas Heimreise, 192, 203-04; Elektra, 19, 109, 173, 194-204, 220, 228; Die Frau im Fenster, 191; Die Frau ohne Schatten (libretto), 19, 85, 109, 173, 192-93, 199, 203; 204-09, 214, 225-26, 241; Gestern, 5, 51-52, 75, 79, 87, 106-09, 113, 191; Die Hochzeit der Sobeide, 191; Der

Kaiser und die Hexe, 191; <u>König Odipus</u>, 204; <u>Das kleine Welttheater</u>, 40-42, 121; <u>Odipus und die Sphinx</u>, 204; <u>Der Rosenkavalier</u>, 35, 192, 203-04; <u>Der Schwierige</u>, 192, 228; <u>Silvia im "Stern"</u>, 204; <u>Der Tod des Tizian</u>, 19, 86, 106, 109-12, 114, 117, 120, 126; <u>Der Tor und der Tod</u>, 45, 87, 106, 109, 112-15, 127; <u>Der Turm</u> (1927), 147, 205, 228; <u>Der weiße Fächer</u>, 196.

Hugo, Victor, 149

Huysmans, Joris-Karl, 7-8, 101

Joyce, James, 144

Kahn, Gustave, 3

Kant, Immanuel, 99

Keats, John, 59, 65

Laforgue, Jules, 3

Lenau, Nikolaus, 229

Lucretius, 124

Maeterlinck, Maurice, 15, 75, 77, 146

Malherbe, Francois de, 159

Mallarmé, Stéphane, 2-3, 5-6, 8-10, 12-14, 16, 18-19, 28, 43-45, 47-51, 54-55, 60, 62, 64-66, 72, 76-79, 88, 99, 103-04, 118, 137, 142-45, 148-49, 159, 161, 170-91, 201, 204, 209-11, 220-21, 228-29, 240

    Scène" from "Hérodiade," 19, 44, 76-79, 103, 170-91, 201-02, 204, 209-14, 216-17, 220-21, 223-25, 228-29

Mann, Thomas, 103, 207

Maupassant, Guy de, 8

Mauron, Charles, 190

Meyer, Conrad Ferdinand, 58

Mitterwurzer, Friedrich, 53, 55

Mörike, Eduard, 58

Montesquiou, Robert de, 176

Moréas, Jean, 3

Morris, William, 101

Nietzsche, Friedrich, 121

Noulet, Emilie, 78

Novalis (Friedrich von Hardenberg), 88, 149

Ortega y Gasset, José, 193, 240-42

Otway, Thomas, 194

Pater, Walter, 101, 124

Pestalozzi, Karl, 53

Platen, August Graf von, 61

Poe, Edgar Allan, 12, 14, 118, 137

Pound, Ezra, 238, 242

Poussin, Nicolas, 1

Praz, Mario, 169, 178, 182, 191-92, 199

Racine, Jean, 59

Régnier, Henri de, 159

Richard, Jean-Pierre, 43-45, 183

Rilke, Rainer Maria, 62, 73-74

Rimbaud, Arthur, 159

Rossetti, Dante Gabriel, 14

Rubens, Peter Paul, 1

Ruskin, John, 100-01, 125, 237

Saas, Christa, 80-81

St. Aubyn, F. C., 209-10

Saint-Paul, Albert, 13
Schiller, Friedrich, 46, 61, 99, 102, 203
Schnitzler, Arthur, 10
Shelley, Percy Bysshe, 14
Sondrup, Steven P., 17
Sophocles, 194-97, 199
Staiger, Emil, 55-58, 74
Steiner, Herbert, 84
Strauss, Richard, 204-05, 207
Swinburne, Algernon Charles, 14, 101, 118-24, 126, 128-29
Szondi, Peter, 52, 77, 79, 106, 108, 113, 181, 184, 188, 192
Thompson, Stith, 211
Valéry, Paul, 15, 72, 137
Verlaine, Paul, 2-3, 5-6, 8-10, 12, 14, 16-17, 59-60, 62-65, 72, 99, 118, 134
Vielé-Griffin, Francis, 16-17, 64, 134-35
Villiers de l'Isle-Adam, P. H., 7, 75, 175
Villon, Francois, 35
Weisstein, Ulrich, 72
Whistler, James McNeil, 101
Wilde, Oscar, 1, 101-02, 106, 119, 152, 190
Willoughby, L. A., 102
Wimsatt, W. K., 56-58
Winckelmann, Johann Joachim, 46
Wordsworth, William, 58
Ziolkowski, Theodore, 144

Alexander Woronzoff

ANDREJ BELYJ'S *PETERSBURG,* JAMES JOYCE'S *ULYSSES* AND THE SYMBOLIST MOVEMENT

American University Studies III (Comparative Literature), vol. 1
X, 215 pages   paperback $ 21.05

This book is an analysis of Joyce's and Belyj's appropriation and adaptation of symbolist poetic devices in the novels *Ulysses* and *Petersburg.* Of central importance is Joyce's use of epiphany and Belyj's use of the aesthetic symbol. They are units of meaning that create countless associations by expanding to ever widening areas of significance and then returning upon themselves. To achieve a structure based on epiphany and symbol, Joyce and Belyj make use of devices such as the creation of correspondences through metaphorical analogy, interior monologue and stream of consciousness, synesthesia, musical effects and refrain, leitmotif, linguistic and technical virtuosity, and an allusive construction.

Maurice R. Funke

FROM SAINT TO PSYCHOTIC: THE CRISIS OF HUMAN IDENTITY IN THE LATE 18TH CENTURY
A Comparative Study of Clarissa, La Nouvelle Héloise. Die Leiden des jungen Werthers

American University Studies III (Comparative Literature), vol. 2
220 pages   paperback $ 20.55

As the literary historian moves from *Clarissa* through *La Nouvelle Héloise* to *Werther,* he sees concepts which had hitherto been accepted as constants within the matrix of human values being put into question. The very idea of man's ability to know the truth emerges as an assumption based upon acquired knowledge rather than actual fact. The individual's struggle with what by societal conventions has been established as natural erodes his self confidence and even his individuality is identified as role playing. The attempt at self-definition leads the tormented individual to rely upon a transcendent principle which to provide security but which actually arises out of scepticism and sexual guilt. Suicide, the act of incorporating death into the concept of personal identity, constitutes the most extreme form of this struggle.

PETER LANG PUBLISHING, INC.
34 East 39th Street
USA – New York, NY 10016

Carol Wootton
SELECTIVE AFFINITIES
Comparative Essays from Goethe to Arden

American University Studies III (Comparative Literature), vol. 3
183 pages   paperback $ 17.35

The aim of this series of essays is to show the attraction of certain authors, themes and movements in German literature and to explore their sometimes surprising affinities with a number of writers and their concerns in the English-speaking world. Composers, too, are introduced to reveal the diversity of Comparative Literature studies.
Contents: Goethe and Yeats – Shaw and Wedekind – Romantic Irony and Music – Hofmannsthal and Eliot – Ferruccio Busoni and Faust – Gottfried Benn and Chopin – Benn and Sylvia Plath – The Götz of Goethe and John Arden.

PETER LANG PUBLISHING, INC.
34 East 39th Street
USA – New York, NY 10016